WILDERNESS COOKING

To our daughter Kim

WILDERNESS COOKING

A unique illustrated cookbook and guide for outdoor enthusiasts

By
Berndt Berglund
and
Clare E. Bolsby

Illustrated by E. B. Sanders

CHARLES SCRIBNER'S SONS
NEW YORK

Printed in the United States

ISBN No. 0-684-14715-7 Paper

PREFACE

This book about wilderness cooking has been created mainly for people who like to get out in the wilderness with a minimum of packing.

To live off the land requires experience and planning. Many of the recipes in this book have been adapted from century old Indian, trapper and pioneer traditions handed down through the generations.

Cookery is not only an art, but a science as well. To cook economically is an art, which had to be practiced by early settlers and lonely trappers in the wilderness, where no store-bought supplies could be obtained for months on end.

It was an absolute necessity to gather and preserve food either from the wilderness or the home vegetable garden.

The Indians had for many thousands of years utilized whatever was available in the bush, and of course the early pioneers soon learned from them what was edible and what was not — plant or animal.

As settlers arrived from all parts of the world, their eating habits and old Indian customs merged to become an entirely new diet, suitable to the climate and supplies available in the New World.

Many of the old recipes and methods have been lost in our modern way of life with new methods of preserving foods by canning and freeze-drying. We have tried to carefully select and modernize these century-old recipes without changing the contents and the methods of preparation. It has however, been necessary to convert weights and measures to modern standards. Also, it is a good idea to remember that adjustments may have to be made in some of these recipes, particularly in those containing baking powder, when you are cooking at high altitudes.

Almost anyone can cook well with a wide range of ingredients on hand, but the real science of cooking is to be able to cook a good meal with little from which to make it. That is what our book will help you to do, we hope.

The Authors

Simplified Measurements Often Used by
Woodsmen and Guides

"Handful" — the quantity obtained by using the hand as a scoop, filling it as full as possible.

"Two fingers", or "three fingers" — these measures are used for dry materials such as baking powder, etc. Use the number of fingers called for. Hold them close together. Dip into the material and lift out with the fingers and thumb without turning the hand.

"One finger of fat" — use your little finger as a scoop and scoop out as much fat as will stay in the bend of your little finger.

"One cup" — woodsmen usually make sure that their drinking cup holds just about one measuring cup.

Wildwood Seasoning

Coltsfoot Salt, Spice Bush, Wild Mint, Wild Ginger, Wintergreen, Sweet Bay, Cherry Birch, Indian Vinegar, and Wild Mustard are mentioned and used in many recipes throughout the book. See Chapter 13 for detailed description.

CONTENTS

Chapter 1

HISTORY OF WILDERNESS COOKING

Fire dates back to the dawn of man. It is known that the Peking man, some 500,000 years ago had fire at his disposal, but it is not known when the cooking of food began. But one thing is certain; when man started to cook food, it greatly varied his diet.

We differentiate between cooking and cookery. Cooking is simply applying heat to food materials, but cookery is the art of food preparation.

In the wilderness the most-used method of food preparation is cooking, but I have met many wilderness cooks who have developed simple wilderness cooking to a high degree of cookery.

Wilderness cooking has to adapt itself to how you travel, and to the length of time you stay in one place.

It can be simply heating water over a small fire for a cup of tea, or it may involve preparations for a winter's stay at your camp or cabin. The Indians were masters of these methods and pioneers soon learned from them how to utilize our wilderness supply of produce and game.

Corn, squash, potatoes and tomatoes are only a few examples of what the North American Indian introduced to the early settler's diet. Habit and nostalgia played their part in early wilderness cooking. Conservatism in taste and many mixed cultures blended together in pioneer methods of preserving and cooking.

Many century old dishes had to be simplified and streamlined to fit into the travelling scout's and frontiersman's packsack.

Most of the cooking had to be done over open fires along the trail. But even with very simple methods, many a gourmet dish was created at this time.

Of course, the most important consideration was to travel light with a minimum of staples, but nevertheless what was carried, had to be nourishing and wholesome to give the traveller strength for the often long and arduous journeys.

Much time was spent by the Indians and pioneers collecting and preparing food for the long, cold winter days when snow made it impossible to travel any distance at all. Much ingenuity went into preparing meat and greens so that they would keep until spring, when supplies of fresh vegetables and meat could be acquired again.

Also, it is true to say that to the early settlers and bushmen, cooking was an art in economy.

A careless cook could waste more food than a man could carry on his back. In the pioneer days, cooks never wasted anything that could be used.

There were many recipes where the whole animal was used down to the last bit of scrap. A lot of ingredients had to be improvised, but in many cases the improvisation improved the dish. Nothing was known of today's sophisticated food technology, but nevertheless their diet was often well balanced to include carbohydrates, fats, proteins and water.

Many recipes included in this book will probably seem farfetched to you, but we can assure you that they have been used for generations with good results.

The recipes quite often require a great deal of time to make, but as time was of no consequence to the frontierswoman, we must be prepared to spend equal time to recreate these dishes.

Chapter 2

HUNTING AND FISHING

It may seem unusual to you that a cookbook should contain information about killing or catching fish. But we have found that many people who travel in the bush do not have any idea of how to get the food which they might need, so we feel justified in discussing the initial steps of securing food for the pot.

Hunting with Bow and Arrow

The bow and arrow was one of the first tools man used to kill game, after the stone or the club proved inadequate. Today bow hunting has taken on a new popularity.

Archery is not a test of strength, but a test of skill and to be able to enjoy shooting, the skill must be acquired. As with all sports, skill can only be acquired by practice. There is no short cut which will eliminate the need for practice. Success lies in the ability to do the same thing, the same way, every time. Needless to say, for the animal's sake you should *never* attempt to hunt with bow and arrow until you have acquired sufficient skill.

Remember that archery is a very personal sport and every archer is different in physical build, bone structure, nervous system, reflexes, etc. It is absolutely necessary that you have the right equipment and that you know and understand this equipment.

We suggest that you seek the advice of an expert as there are some things only he can help you with. An awareness of the six basic aspects of archery will help you to learn to do the same thing, the same way every time; in other words, to develop rhythm.

1. Stance
2. Nocking the arrow
3. Drawing and anchor
4. Holding and aiming
5. Releasing
6. Follow through

A good book on archery will carry you through these rules step by step, but the help of an expert archer will benefit you more.

It is vitally important that you know how to select your equipment. Many an archer-to-be has given up this interesting sport just because he purchased the wrong equipment.

Of course it is important that you make up your mind what kind of shooting you intend to do, as the equipment varies. But as this book is concerned with game, we will talk about equipment for bow hunting.

Any bow used for hunting should have a draw weight of not less than forty pounds, this being the number of pounds pull required to draw a twenty eight inch arrow to its head and to project an arrow 150 yards.

Any arrow used for hunting shall be tipped with either a sharp broadhead point of not less than one inch in width or a sharp bodkin type three-bladed point. The use of an arrow twenty four inches or less is prohibited in most states and provinces.

Most archers wear camouflage clothing to be able to approach their prey as closely as possible. It is important to move almost soundlessly in the bush in order to have any success in bow hunting.

An old Indian guide told me to always stay on the north side of a ridge when hunting, because you can usually travel without making a sound on the soft damp ground where the sun has not dried out the grass and fallen branches.

The art of stalking game was practised to perfection by the Indians. I have seen some of my Indian guides approach game so closely that they could almost touch it.

Here are a few tips to remember when stalking game.

Always determine the direction of the wind. If the wind is low, pick up a handful of dirt or dried leaves and let them drift slowly to the ground to detect the direction of the wind.

Most animals in the bush depend on their acute sense of smell to warn them of danger. Always make sure that you approach them with the wind in your face.

Never smoke when trailing or stalking game; the smoke may be carried miles downrange and scare your game away.

Always wear moccasins or soft soled shoes. If you get used to moccasins, you can literally feel your way with your feet. When you are travelling in rocky terrain, set your toes down first, and when travelling in grass, set your heels down first.

Always be sure to travel under cover. Never expose yourself, and keep close to the earth. Never break over a ridge without first having scouted the other side from behind a bush or tree. Put grass or a few branches in your hat so that you blend in with your surroundings.

Never let your shadow project behind your shelter. Its movement is a dead giveaway. Try to match your clothes to the color of your background. If stalking game in the snow, wear white clothing and beware of shadows on the snow.

When close to your game it may be necessary to crawl on the ground. This is something to practice; learn to crawl on the ground with your weapon held high and free from dirt.

Indians frequently used animal pelts to get close to their prey. Decoys were often made out of rushes. I was participating in a hunt for waterfowl in northern Canada one year and our Indian guide made several dozen decoys out of grass and rushes. These were better than any other decoys I had ever used.

Snares and Traps

Indians often used snares and traps to collect their game. One advantage of this kind of hunting is that you can set many snares at a time and have a greater chance of success. But it is essential that you look after the traps often, not only to collect the game, but most important to spare the animal from unnecessary hardship. Also, trapped animals may scare away other animals if left in the trap.

Hunting with Firearms

The more time you spend in the area where you intend to hunt to find game trails, natural crossings, marshes and water holes, the more successful your hunt is going to be. If you are going to an unfamiliar area, seek the advice and guidance of a qualified authority.

16

One mistake which many hunters make is to ignore the advice of local guides. After all, they have a working knowledge of their area and many years of hunting in the same district have given them inside information about game behavior in that area. They know where game is usually found and you can be sure that they will do their best to make your hunt a success. Do your share of work around the camp and obey the guide's instructions about safety precautions.

The best time of day to scout the district where you are going to hunt is in the morning and evening when game is astir to gather food and water.

Open pastures or along the edges of marshes and streams are logical places to look for big game. When tracking or stalking, walk slowly and stop to listen frequently. Seemingly, animals are less alarmed at the sound of a man who ambles through the bush stopping occasionally, than at the noise of one who continually stomps through the bush with a heavy regular step. Remember, animals can hear you walking miles away.

Be observant; a deer or a moose will let you come quite close without moving. Watch for the flicker of an ear, the move of a hoof, or the wag of a tail. I have seen hunters walk by a deer an arm's length away without seeing it. The cry of a bluejay or magpie in the distance often betrays the presence of game.

Before entering an open area in the bush, creep carefully to a vantage point where you can scan the open track ahead of you from a well-concealed spot. Spend some time closely examining the opposite bush. In many instances you will find that this procedure will pay off in the long run. In all hunting, make it your objective to get as close as you can before firing a shot.

Try to place your shot in a vital area: heart, neck or brain. Hits in other parts of the body might drop the animal, but as you approach, it might take off, badly injured. If you have only wounded your game, sit down and wait for 15 or 20 minutes. This will give the animal false security and it will stop running, lie down and usually stiffen, so that you will be able to catch up.

As far as guns go, it's a matter of personal taste, but after thirty years of experience in the bush, the following are my companions on the trail.

An all-round heavy calibre gun, good for hunting moose, deer and bear is the 30-06 Winchester bolt action rifle. The reason I prefer this gun is because the bolt action is more dependable and there is less chance that it will jam in a critical situation. This gun has fewer moving parts, the bolt has a positive lock and it gives you maximum leverage to load and unload. It is easy to repair and simple to take down for cleaning.

The 30-06 caliber also offers a wider selection of bullet weights capable of handling most small and big game found in North America although I would think twice before firing a shot at an angry grizzly.

My second, or back-up rifle, is the Winchester 30-30 lever action although more care has to be taken to keep this gun clean and free from dirt.

For hunting small game, waterfowl and birds I trust my over-under 12-gauge Winchester shotgun. It is simple in construction, easy to keep clean and it never seems to wear out. I have found that two shots are plenty. If the first shot misses, or you wound the game, the second shot from the modified choked barrel will usually bring down the bird.

I never use a hand gun for hunting. Personally, I feel the handgun is an inadequate short range gun, not at home in the bush where your life may depend on the game you kill.

The selection of guns is a very personal matter, but bear in mind when you buy a gun, to choose one which suits you and which will serve you for many years. Select one made by a reliable manufacturer, even if it means spending a few more dollars. It will cost less in maintenance and spare parts.

Chapter 3

FIELD DRESSING OF GAME

BIG GAME

It's a fact that more perfectly good meat is spoiled in the bush than is ruined by incompetent cooks. Much of the big game taken out of our wilderness is spoiled while draped over the hood or fender of a car. Heat from the motor will spoil meat rapidly.

Usually the game has not been properly cleaned, and in most cases, no attempt to skin the animal has been made. It may be less spectacular to come home with the game properly cleaned, skinned and quartered, than to drive down the highway with the whole animal mounted on the car fender to show what a great hunter you are.

Nine times out of ten, irreparable damage has been done to the meat before the cook has even had a chance to prepare it. Unfortunately, it is the cook's reputation that suffers.

The first rule of the kill is to dress the game immediately. Experienced trappers and Indians always skin and clean an animal on the spot where it was killed.

Furthermore, a large animal cut-up is much easier to carry out of the bush than a whole animal.

It is very important that the dead animal be hung to cool and this cannot be done without first removing the skin so that fresh air can circulate freely around the carcass. If you are not sure how to cut up the animal, halve it or quarter it and bring it to a reliable butcher or meat packing plant. In other words, leave it to the experts.

To do a good job of dressing your game you will need an adequate hunting knife with a five inch blade, a belt axe to split collapsible heavy bones, and a saw for cutting-up big game. To keep your tools sharp, you should always carry a sharpening stone. Make sure that you know how to use the stone so as to keep your knife and axe in razor-sharp condition.

Thirty feet of strong nylon rope will come in handy to hoist a heavy carcass into a tree. Use strong, absorbent paper towels to clean out the cavity, then rub coarse salt and black pepper into the meat to keep flies and insects away. Several yards of cheesecloth can be used to wrap around the carcass, but this is not necessary.

Of course, before you start any of these preparations, make sure that the animal is dead. But don't approach it from any other direction than from the rear. Then use your knife to prick one of the hind legs.

By the way, most state and provincial laws require that the animal be tagged as soon as it is killed; also be careful not to destroy evidence of sex.

BLEEDING

Many people contend that with today's high velocity ammunition, bleeding the animal is unnecessary. They may be right, but every hunter and trapper I have ever met holds as I do, that to retain the sweet taste of the meat it is absolutely necessary to bleed game as soon as it has been killed.

Place the animal on a slant with the hind legs high. Insert your hunting knife at the top of the breastbone with the point of the knife aimed toward the backbone, then withdraw the knife with a slight cutting motion. This will sever the carotid arteries where they join midway between the shoulders.

There will be a fair amount of blood drained off by gravity and if you can

20

rig up a tripod to raise the rear portion of the animal, so much the better. If you intend to keep the head for mounting, tilt the head back and tie the antlers in this position to keep the head free from blood stains.

While you wait for the blood to drain, cut off the musk glands on the hind legs. Deer have musk glands on the inside as well as the outside of each leg. Musk glands can be identified by a heavy tuft of upraised hair, growing in oval patches around them.

Carefully remove them; try not to touch them with your hands. Dispose of them and wash your hands and knife thoroughly. If water is not available, make a small fire and insert the blade of the knife in the flames several times but don't get it so hot that it changes the temper of the blade. As for your hands, rub them well with earth or moss to get them as clean as possible. This will protect the meat from being tainted by the musk odor.

DRESSING

When most of the blood has drained, put the carcass down on the ground and roll it over on its back with the rump lower than the head. Spread the hind legs as far apart as possible. If you are alone, it is a good idea to secure one of the legs with a rope to a tree to give you a free hand when opening the cavity.

Open the carcass from crotch to throat, being extremely careful not to puncture the intestines or pouch. One way to do this is to hold the intestines away from the knife by inserting the hand between the sac and the hide.

After cutting through the hide and scraping against the breastbone, the cutting edge of your knife will be dull and it is wise to hone it before going any further.

With your sharp knife, cut around the anus and draw it into the body cavity so it comes free together with the intestines. Watch so that you don't cut into or break the bladder. With your hands, loosen the stomach and intestines from the body, and roll them out on the ground. Locate and save the liver.

Reach forward and with the knife, cut around the diaphragm which separates the lungs and the stomach. Free lungs from the body with your hands. Reach forward and cut the windpipe and gullet in front of the lungs. Pull out lungs and heart from the chest cavity and save the heart.

Drain all the blood and wipe the cavity clean with the paper towels you have in your gear.

If you were unlucky and placed the shot in the stomach or lungs, you must wash the cavity out with clean water, but this only applies if the cavity is badly damaged.

SKINNING

Many people believe that it is much easier to skin an animal when it is hanging, but I prefer to do the skinning with the animal lying on the ground.

Start to skin by cutting the hide around the neck. If you intend to save the head for a trophy, make this cut at the shoulders.

Cut along the inside of each leg from the cavity opening to the first joint. Cut the shanks about an inch and a half below the hook. Up to this point your skinning knife has been necessary, but you don't need it any more.

Use your hands and grab the pelt with one hand pulling outwards and the other hand forcing the pelt away from the carcass. This method will free the hide from the flesh and save it from unnecessary cuts from your knife. Lightly salt the flesh side of the hide and roll it up for a day or two. This will help to loosen the hair. If you intend to tan the hide, tack it up on a wall or other flat surface, making sure that you don't over-stretch it. Remove all excess flesh and tallow that might be clinging to the hide.

Don't fold the hide at any time as the folds will always show, even after tanning.

AGING MEAT

Before the carcass is butchered and wrapped for storage, the meat should be hung for 10 to 12 days in a well-ventilated area at a temperature of 35 to 40 degrees F. This procedure is most important as it ripens or ages the meat. This age-old method of breaking down the fibres in the meat is often neglected by butchers today. When aged, meat takes on a dark red color which makes it difficult to sell over the counter, as most people think it is spoiled.

Delicious tender steaks served in a good restaurant or steakhouse are cut from meat that has been properly aged. Another secret is to pound steaks with a heavy mallet to tenderize them even more. Meat for your own table should get the same consideration and care.

SMALL GAME

Animals that are considered small game include beaver, muskrat, rabbit, squirrel, woodchuck and groundhog.

These animals should be skinned and cleaned as soon as possible after death. Do remember that it is much easier to skin a small carcass before the innards are removed.

Hunters often save the skins, so care should be taken not to damage them. Slit the skin on the inside of the hind legs from the paws to the vent and cut off both hind legs, front legs and the tail. Work the skin off inside out, using your knife as little as possible and take special care around the eyes and lips.

If the skin is to be saved, scrape off all fat and flesh and roll the pelt for proper care later in camp.

Remove the head from the carcass. Open the animal by inserting the knife blade, sharp edge up, at the tip of the breast bone. Cut through the thin meat over the belly being very careful not to puncture the entrails. Encircle the vent and spread the cavity open. Remove the entrails by grasping above the stomach and pulling down and out from the body cavity. Remove the heart and lungs and with a sharp knife remove the musk glands on animals that have them.

Fill the cavity with small fresh branches of juniper or any other available evergreen.

BIRDS

All hunters have their own methods of caring for their game. This is the way we usually do it.

Many men prefer to carry birds all day during the hunt, but I have found that if the bird is cleaned when it is still warm, it makes the job very much easier.

Pluck a strip of feathers along the breastbone to the vent with your hunting knife. Make a shallow cut along this strip encircling the vent. But remember, the skin is very thin and you can easily puncture the intestines. Insert two fingers through this opening and reach up as far as possible. Then rotate your hand to loosen all the organs and bring the intestines out. Make sure the lungs are there too. If not, reach carefully up and loosen them, but be careful of tiny bone fragments splintered by shot; they can cut fingers like a razor blade.

Turn the bird over and make a cut along the front of the neck. Remove the crop and the windpipe. Separate and save the giblets (liver, heart and gizzard).

Place fresh evergreen boughs or grass in the cavity and try to hang the bird in the shade until you go back to camp. Birds should hang, as well as game, to age, the length of time depending on the individual's taste for strong or mild flavored meat.

I prefer to dry-pluck game birds even if it is time consuming, as the dry skin protects the flavor and moistness of the meat. Birds should be plucked as soon as they have been cleaned and while they are still warm, to make the job as easy as possible. Remember to save one wing with wing plumage for identification by the authorities.

Plucking feathers seems to be fairly easy if you pull downwards in the direction they are growing. This will protect the skin from being torn. Start to remove the feathers from the back, then the breast, ending up at the first joint of the leg and wings. Chop off the head about an inch from the body.

If any down or pinfeathers remain, take care of this back at camp by either searing the bird with a small flame, or pouring melted paraffin over the bird. When the wax has hardened, it will scrape off with a dull knife taking pinfeathers with it. The last thing to do before hanging the bird is to cut out the oil sacs which are located on either side of the backbone just above the tail.

FISH

The same meticulous care must be taken with fresh fish as with any other meat to protect its delicious flavor. First and foremost, clean fish as soon as they are caught.

When ice-fishing, dip the cleaned fish in the water at sufficient intervals to allow the fish to be coated with a thin layer of ice. This will prevent the sun's rays or bitter cold from drying the skin.

In warm weather fish must be kept out of the sun and preferably in a cooler with ice. The summer heat will cause the flesh to deteriorate very quickly, so don't leave fish lying in the bottom of the boat. Along with your other equipment, plan on taking your ice-cooler with you in the boat. It's just as necessary as the rest of your fishing gear. Never, never, drag fish behind a boat on a stringer unless you like them impregnated with gasoline and oil. Don't forget that it is important to remove the gills as well as the entrails.

Scaling fish should be done as soon as possible because the longer you leave it, the harder it is to do.

Place the fish on a board and hold the tail firmly with one hand. With the other hand, pull a dull knife or scaler from tail to head, against the scales at a forty-five degree angle. If you can manage to do this under water, the scales will not fly about so much. Always scale from the tail towards the head on both sides leaving the back until last.

Now, insert the tip of the knife at the vent and slit the skin along the center line of the belly ending by cutting out the gills. Take a good hold of the gills and pull backwards toward the tail to remove the gill attachment and the entrails.

Cut around the vent to free the intestines. Remove the blood streak along the spine with the tip of your knife and your thumb. Remove the head by cutting across the base of the gills. If the backbone is large, cut through the flesh on either side of it and with the head over the edge of the board, snap it off.

To remove the fins, cut on each side of them, then grab the fins firmly and pull sharply towards the head to loosen the root bones.

Chapter 4

BUTCHERING OF BIG GAME

Animals considered to be big game include bear, buffalo, caribou, Dahl sheep, elk, deer, moose and reindeer.

Cutting the Meat

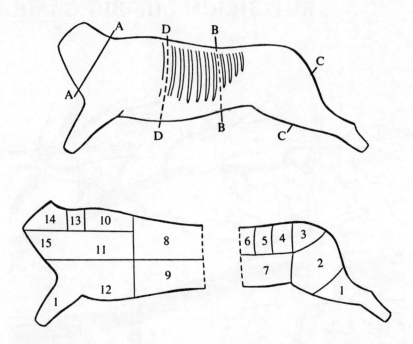

Most hunters take their game to a professional butcher to be cut and wrapped for the freezer. This is the best idea if you don't know how to do it yourself. But in some instances out in the bush, you have to depend on your own knowledge to do this important job.

Hang the carcass by the hooks with a spreader between the legs. Use a meat saw and cut the carcass in half down the back bone. Take one half at a time and cut it up according to the diagram. Make sure that your butcher knife is sharp and that the meat cleaver is heavy enough to do the job.

Place the carcass inside down on the cutting table. Cut off the neck along the line A-A. Put it to the side. Sever the carcass along the line B-B which is just in front of the second rib from the back and saw through the backbone. Remove the hind legs by cutting along the line C-C in the diagram. Now move forward and remove the shoulder and front legs by cutting along the line D-D. Start the cut between the fifth and sixth rib and follow the line D.

The basic cuts are done. Now take time to clean and cut away all mutilated or bloody areas from the large cuts and put them in a weak brine solution of a quarter pound of table salt in a gallon of lukewarm water. The salt will draw the blood and the meat will be ready for stewing or grinding in 24 hours.

The larger pieces of meat can now be cut into the desired cuts, wrapped and frozen for future use. To help the beginner with this chore, we have prepared a comprehensive diagram.

Fig. 1	Fore and hind shanks are usually used for stewing beef or hamburger.
Fig. 2	Round steak is usually tender and is used for steaks or roasts.
Fig. 3	The rump is very good as a roast or a pot roast.
Fig. 4	The sirloin is used for steaks.
Fig. 5	This section is cut into porterhouse steaks.
Fig. 6	Wing steaks come from this section.
Fig. 7	The flank is usually used for stewing beef or hamburger but can be thinned out for flank steaks.
Fig. 8 and 9	Rib roasts come from the middle of the carcass but many people like to cut this meat for rolled brisket.
Fig. 10	This section is the blade roast or it can be cut up for pot roasts or corning.
Fig. 11	The short rib roast comes from the chuck.
Fig. 12	This is the brisket. It is tender after the tendons are removed and is used for stew, ground meat and roasts.
Fig. 13	This section is the chuck roast and is one of the tastiest cuts of meat.
Fig. 14 and 15	This cut usually goes into shoulder roasts or stew or ground meat.

Mark each package as it is wrapped, or you may forget what is in it by the time you are finished with the whole animal.

SMALL GAME

Very small game is usually skinned and cooked whole or cut up for a stew.

Medium size game can be cut up in much the same way as large game depending on the size of your pot and your recipe.

First, cut off the head and then remove the shoulders and legs. It is usually a good idea to cut the legs into two pieces but it depends on the size of the animal. Cut away the flanks and the neck and split each in two. What you have left is the breast and the loin. Separate and cut into normal serving pieces, not too small. Remember that meat will shrink while cooking.

Small game is usually more difficult to cut up than large game and the beginner often spoils the finished product with too small pieces.

The main thing to remember is to cut up your game in such a way that no meat is spoiled and discarded.

Chapter 5

CURING OF GAME AND FISH

Salt and a solution of salt and water have been used by man as far back as our records go, for curing fish and game.

An indication of this is the common word 'salary' which comes from the Latin word *salarium*, or money allowed the soldiers for the purchase of salt. At one time salt was a high-priced trading commodity widely used by our Indians.

Fish dipped in a salt solution will last a long time. This was the only way that Indians and early settlers could keep meat and fish during the summer months. Even today you will find the same method being used by lonely trappers in our wilderness.

Game meat can be preserved for almost any length of time without refrigeration if you follow any of these recipes. Quantities are based on 100 pounds of meat.

7 pounds salt	**1 quart dark molasses**
1 ounce saltpeter	**8 gallons water**
1 ounce cayenne pepper	

Rub the meat with coarse salt and place it in a container large enough to hold all the meat and brine. Let stand for 24 hours to draw the blood from the meat. Remove the meat and drain. Scald the container with boiling water and repack the meat.

Bring water to a boil and add remaining ingredients. Skim off suds as the solution boils. Remove from heat and cool.

When brine is cool, pour over the meat to cover completely. The container should be earthenware or an oak cask.

The following method was used by Indians out West for preserving meat and for a dipping solution before drying meat.

6 pounds salt	**Cold water to cover meat**

Cut game into medium size pieces. Sprinkle about one-third of the salt over the bottom of a barrel or crock. Pack meat without salt. Pour remaining salt over top of meat; then add water.

Using this method, meat will keep a long time and will taste as fresh as the day it was packed.

If the meat is designed to be dried, let it stand in the brine for about three weeks. Remove the meat from the brine and soak in fresh cold water overnight to wash off excess salt. Hang in the sun to dry.

Once, when visiting an old trapper in the middle of the summer, he served me bacon and eggs for breakfast. Knowing he was about 15 days from the nearest store, I was curious about his supply of fresh bacon.

He explained that as soon as he gets a piece of cured bacon, he slices it the thickness he prefers and fries it slightly. Then it is packed in its own fat in small jars and stored. He added that fat-free bacon needs additional lard for proper packing and there must be no air bubbles left in the jar; the juices must fill every nook and cranny. He ties several layers of cheesecloth over the mouth of each jar before the lid goes on. The jars are stored in a cool place.

This recipe was given to me by an eighty year-old prospector who had done his share of hunting and trapping. He was very fond of bear hams and he adopted the following procedure for each one hundred pounds of meat.

4 gallons water	**2 pounds dark brown sugar**
8 pounds coarse salt	**1¼ ounce potash**
2 ounces saltpeter	

Rub bear meat with coarse salt and let stand in a barrel for two days. Then rinse off with lukewarm water and let dry. In the meantime, bring the water to a boil and add the other four ingredients. Wash out the barrel, repack the bear meat and cover with the brine when it has cooled.

Let stand for 6 weeks but take the meat out of the brine 2 or 3 days before you intend to smoke the hams. The potash will keep the meat from drying out and becoming hard.

Bear hams prepared in this manner are delightful and have a slightly gamy taste.

JERKY

Jerky is dried meat, either beef or other large game, cut in long strips about an inch thick and sun dried. Meat treated in this way is easy to carry and lasts a long time.

An Indian guide told me how his forefathers carried jerky with them on extended hunting trips. When the first pangs of hunger hit, an Indian hunter put a piece of jerky between himself and the horse and bounced on it for a while to soften it. When he judged it to be the desired softness, he would take a bite and chew his dinner as he hunted. In this way the hunter could pursue his game without stopping to cook a meal.

I have had uncooked jerky, very thinly sliced, on bread and found it to be almost as good as smoked meat.

To prepare sun-dried jerky, cut fresh meat into long thin strips about an inch wide and an inch thick. Rub the strips with salt or garlic and hang, well spaced on racks, in the sun to dry as quickly as possible. Store in sacks hung in a dry place.

Jerky can also be made by placing the strips in a corning solution for three or four days, then hung on racks in the sun over a slow burning, smoky fire for at least 48 hours. It is important to keep the strips from touching each other and they should be wrapped in cheesecloth to keep dirt and insects from settling on the meat.

Jerky will continue to dry as long as it is exposed to air and smoke, so it is important not to leave it longer than 48 hours. Then store it in air-tight containers.

This recipe is a tasty corning solution for about fifty pounds of meat.

3 gallons water	**1 ounce cayenne pepper**
2 pounds dark brown sugar	**1 cup juniper berries, crushed**
1 ounce saltpeter	**1 whole piece ginger**

Bring water to a boil and add remaining ingredients. Boil for five minutes, removing scum as it appears. Cool and store in a wooden barrel or earthenware crock.

FISH

Early in the spring when the fish were running, Indians and early settlers usually filled their larders with fresh fish but it posed quite a problem to keep the fish edible for long periods of time. Here is how they solved the problem.

The settlers prepared large barrels by steaming them clean and putting a layer of coarse salt on the bottom. As the fish were cleaned, they were carefully set in the barrels with alternate layers of onion and salt until they were filled to the brim and the lid was as tight as possible.

The fish became very salty of course, but soaking each one in cold water overnight lessened the salty flavor.

On special occasions fish were simmered in milk or cream, a meal fit for a king. Larger fish were cut open along the belly, head and backbone were removed, but not through the skin. Each half was liberally sprinkled with coarse salt and maple sugar or brown sugar. Lots of freshly cut dill was used, almost as stuffing, then the halves were folded together again and put in a specially made wooden box just large enough to accommodate the fish. An oak board was placed on top of the fish and pressed down by heavy weights. The boxes were then stored in a cool place.

A beautiful marinade resulted from this procedure. The fish were turned every day so that each half was soaked in the juice for 24 hours. About a week later, the fish were taken out of the marinade, cut in smaller pieces and stored in earthenware crocks in a cool room.

Fish prepared in this way were thinly sliced and eaten with bread.

Chapter 6

WILDERNESS COOKING: INDIAN WAYS

Many Indian tribes used this method to boil water and cook some of their food. The Assiniboine "stone boilers" were a Siouan tribe living between the tree line and the U.S. border and their principal food was buffalo.

This tribe would dig a hole in the ground and peg a buffalo hide over the hole to form a primitive kettle. The hide was then filled with water, meat and greens. Small red-hot stones were dropped into the water to make it boil.

Other tribes used birch bark containers in a similar manner with the same results.

When our family goes camping, we often try this cooking method using either birch bark or more modern materials. The hole is dug big enough to hold the equipment necessary for boiling the water and food to be cooked. A piece of plastic can be used to line the hole, then fill it with water and place four cold stones of similar size in the bottom.

Make a basket out of slender branches and set it in the water on the stones. This basket will hold the hot stones, otherwise they would burn holes in the plastic. Meat and vegetables are placed outside around the basket. As they cool, the cooking stones must be replaced with hot stones to keep the water boiling.

The following recipes are excellent for hot stone cooking.

BEAR STEW ASSINIBOINE

5 pounds bear meat	5 medium dandelion roots, sliced
3 cups maple or birch sap	25 medium arrowhead tubers,
4 cups water	sliced
2 thumbnails coltsfoot salt	1 handful fresh mint leaves
4 wild onions	3 wild leeks, cut up

Trim all fat from the meat and wash well in cold water. Cut the meat into two-inch cubes. Skewer the meat on a sapling and sear on all sides over an open fire. Pour the sap and water into the plastic liner and add remaining ingredients.

Put the sapling basket in the kettle and drop the red hot stones into the basket. As the stones cool, change them to keep the stew simmering for about 45 minutes. Remove the basket and stones and serve the stew as hot as possible.

FRESH CARIBOU TONGUE

1 tongue, medium size	1 handful mint leaves
4 cups water	2 teaspoons coltsfoot salt
2 wild onions, finely chopped	1 cup Indian vinegar

Wash tongue thoroughly with a brush made of evergreen boughs and trim off all stringy muscles.

Put all ingredients in the improvised kettle. Set basket in the kettle and drop in the hot stones until the water boils.

Let the tongue simmer for about 4 hours by continually changing the stones as they cool. Remove the tongue and plunge it into a container of cold water; then remove the skin. Scoop out the liquid in the kettle and strain through several layers of evergreen boughs into a clean container.

Pour the juice over the sliced tongue and eat it hot.

Or, put the tongue back into the strained liquid and set aside to cool for 2 hours. Serve the jellied tongue with slices of corn bread.

RABBIT STEW WITH DUMPLINGS

1 rabbit	1 large dandelion root
2 teaspoons coltsfoot salt	¾ cups flour
Cold water	2 tablespoons baking powder
3 wild onions	½ teaspoon salt
2 handfuls mint	1 egg
15-20 arrowhead tubers	½ cup condensed milk

Cut the skinned and cleaned rabbit into serving pieces. Place in the kettle and add cold water to cover. Put the basket in the kettle and drop in the red hot stones until the water boils. Keep water boiling slowly for an hour by changing the stones as they cool.

Lift the rabbit pieces out of the liquid. Take the meat off the bones and return the meat to the kettle. Add salt, onions, mint, arrowhead and dandelion to the kettle and simmer for another 30 minutes.

For dumplings, mix flour, baking powder and salt. Beat egg and milk together, add dry ingredients and stir just enough to moisten them. Drop the dumpling mixture by the spoonful on the bubbling liquid and cook for another 15 minutes. Remove the basket of stones without disturbing the dumplings.

Stew should sit for about 5 minutes before serving.

GROUNDHOG BROTH WITH WILD RICE

1 large groundhog	1 handful mint, finely chopped
2 tablespoons salt	1 handful black mustard leaves,
2 wild onions finely chopped	finely chopped
3 wild leeks	5 tablespoons flour
Cold water	1 handful wild rice

Take the skinned and cleaned groundhog and cut it into large pieces. Place the pieces in the pot, add the salt and enough cold water to cover the groundhog. Insert the wicker basket and add the red hot stones. Keep it slowly boiling for one hour.

Remove the basket with the hot stones. Take the meat out of the pot and remove all the bones; cut the meat into small pieces and return it to the pot. Add the onions, leeks, mint, wild mustard and wild rice. Replace the wicker basket and bring the broth to a boil. Let boil for 15 minutes.

Remove the stone basket long enough to be able to add the flour that has been mixed with a small amount of cold water. Replace the wicker basket and let boil for another 20 minutes. Serve as hot as possible.

PARTRIDGE STEW

3 partridges	4 wild onions
6 tablespoons bear grease	½ tablespoon coltsfoot salt
1 handful miners lettuce	1 handful mint leaves, finely chopped

Skin and draw the partridge. Wash thoroughly inside and out. Place the partridge on a long stick and brown over the open fire. Baste the partridge with bear grease until it is golden brown.

Place the partridge, the remainder of the bear grease, miners lettuce leaves, onions, coltsfoot salt, and mint in the pot and cover with cold water. Place the stone basket in the pot and add the red hot stones. Bring the water to a boil and by adding more hot stones, keep it at a slow boil for 2 hours stirring once in a while. Thicken the stew with flour, if desired. Serve on hot griddle cakes.

STONE GRIDDLE COOKING

Most modern restaurants or snack bars have a griddle on whose polished surface many dishes are prepared, but don't for a second believe that the griddle is a modern invention.

Indians used a form of griddle, not a shiny piece of steel, but a highly polished flat stone. Their griddles were carefully prepared by smoothing out a piece of sandstone that had been rubbed with gum and tallow. Some of them must have taken weeks on end to finish. They were mainly used to make and to cook cornbread, meat and fish.

You can also make a stone griddle. Select a flat piece of sandstone and place it on four cornerstones, and by brushing and washing the surface, you have made an excellent griddle.

When selecting the flat stone, it is important that you get a piece of sandstone because any other stones when heated may explode into small chips and badly injure the person attending the fire.

A good steady fire of hardwood is essential to get the griddle hot enough to dry out. Take your time and get the griddle dry and clean; it will pay off later.

If you have bear fat or bacon rind, rub it into the griddle and you are ready to use it for your first recipe.

CORNMEAL FLAPJACKS

2 handfuls cornmeal   ¾ cup boiling water
2 fingers salt

Mix the cornmeal and the salt together. Add to the boiling water and make a stiff dough. With well floured hands, make the dough into balls and flatten the balls between your hands. Dip one of your hands in cold water and rub the cake to give it a very smooth surface. Place the cake on the griddle and cook for 10 minutes on each side. Serve hot.

MARINATED PORCUPINE CHOPS

6 porcupine chops   3 fingers coltsfoot salt
1 quart maple sap   4 wild leeks
2 small wild onions

Pour the sap in a birch bark container or other non-metallic container. Cut up the onions into small pieces and add to the sap. Place the porcupine chops one at a time into the solution, placing one wild leek between the chops.

Let stand overnight in a cool place. In the morning grease the stone griddle with fat and remove the chops from the marinade and fry on the griddle. This makes a wonderful breakfast dish if served on hot cornmeal cakes.

TOAD-IN-THE-HOLE

4 pieces white bread   4 eggs
8 slices of bacon   1 finger coltsfoot salt

Place the bacon on the griddle and fry to a crisp. Cut out the center of the bread, leaving a hole in the middle about three and a half inches in diameter. Put the bread on the griddle where the bacon was cooked. Crumble the crisp bacon and drop it in the holes in the bread. Break an egg into each hole, making sure that the white and the yolk stay in the hole. Cook until the egg is fried to your taste. Sprinkle salt over the eggs before serving.

FRIED DRY FISH

1 medium dry fish   3 fingers coltsfoot salt
1 quart maple or birch sap   2 fingers bear or porcupine fat

Place the fish in a birch bark container. Add the sap and let stand overnight. Remove the fish in the morning and leave to drip dry. Grease the stone griddle with the fat and place the fish, skin side down on the griddle. Sprinkle with salt and fry for about 15 minutes. It is important that your griddle be hot. Remove the fish and serve on a piece of birch bark or on a large leaf.

GRILLED MOOSE STEAK

2 large moose steaks, any cut	3 fingers coltsfoot salt
2 large wild onions	2 fingers porcupine fat

Place the moose steaks on a flat clean rock. Pound the steaks with another stone until all the fibers have been broken down. Sprinkle a little coltsfoot salt over the steaks. Cut the wild onions in half and, on the cut side, rub the salt into the meat. Repeat on other side.

Drop the fat on the stone griddle and let it float out over the stone so that you have a well greased spot large enough to place the steaks on. Cook for 15 to 20 minutes on each side. If you have plenty of wild onion, slice the onion thinly and fry it with the steaks.

OPEN RACK SMOKING

Open rack smoking was widely used by Indians to cure meat and fish. This method was an easy way to prepare meat to last for a long time, which of course was important during the spring and summer months when fish and meat spoiled very easily.

Sun drying was probably just as effective, except that clouds and rain could come up suddenly and spoil the drying process.

With the help of heat from a fire, this process was speeded up considerably, and the heavy smoke would not only add a pleasant taste to the meat, but it would also keep flies and insects away from the meat during the drying time.

Smoking racks were made low, often not more than four feet high and placed over a ditch dug in the sand, filled with hardwood branches which gave off a heavy smoke.

Woods such as sugar maple, hickory, beech and juniper were most often used for smoking. It is still a good way to prepare fish and meat, if you are camping in the wilderness too far away from ice and freezing facilities.

The open rack was made as in the illustration. Place two crosses, one in each end, and anchor the cross to the ground with two poles slanted outwards from the cross to the ground and tied to the cross with a piece of string, or a pliable root. Resting on the crosses are slender branches placed parallel with the ditch, and either tied to the cross, or resting on pegs left when cleaning the saplings.

Fish or meat should be smoked in this manner for a couple of days, making sure that the flames do not at any time reach the meat or fish. If the fire gets too hot, sprinkle some water over the coalbed to dampen the flames.

Indians usually just cut up the fish and meat in long strips and hung them on the rack, but I have found that if you cure the fish and the meat for a couple of days in a marinade, and then smoke-cure them, you get a far superior product. The marinade I usually have on hand for such occasions is prepared as follows:

2 gallons maple or birch sap	1 handful coltsfoot salt
4 large wild onions	6 wild leeks
1 handful mint	

Maple or birch sap is placed in a non-metallic container such as birch bark or plastic. The onions, leek and mint are then chopped finely and added to the sap, as well as the salt. The whole thing is heated almost to the boiling point and then removed and cooled, either in a stream or in a hole in the ground.

When the marinade has cooled, put meat or fish into the container and put a piece of bark on top weighted down with a flat stone. Let the meat cure from 2 to 4 days before smoking.

Meat or fish cured in this manner is most palatable and will last for a long time even during the hot summer months.

MUD BAKING

One of the most delightful ways to prepare food by an Indian method is mud baking.

Mud baking provides a wide range of preparing meat, birds and fish in a very tasty way. Of course it is not always possible to do this because you will not always find the right clay or mud for a proper covering. The mud or clay is ideal when you can grab a handful, squeeze it in your hand and it sticks together without cracking or falling apart.

Preparing food this way gives you more free time to spend around camp or to hunt for food, which is important in survival cases.

Furthermore, most of the important juices will be preserved within the food itself. Often a full meal can be prepared and all the ingredients can be included in the mud pack itself. The intermingling of different juices often makes the dish a masterpiece of cookery.

If I am in an area where I can get the right kind of clay, I roll out a sheet of clay to enclose my whole meal. Make the clay sheet about three-quarters of an inch thick and make absolutely certain that there are no holes in the clay. There must be no leak of steam or juice.

If I can't find mud that lends itself to be rolled out in a sheet, I make a container out of bark and line the bottom and sides with mud. Then I place the meat or vegetables inside the container and cover with more mud, making sure that I have all holes plugged before the container is placed in the fire, where the bark is burnt, leaving a solid mud pack.

This system works just as well as the previous method, but it takes more time and greater care has to be taken to protect the food so it will not burn in the fire.

The bird or fish must be drawn and cleaned, but the skin and the feathers may be left on. The head and feet may be cut off, but in many instances if the head is left on, it will improve the taste of the meat.

SQUIRREL WITH JERUSALEM ARTICHOKES

We have two kinds of this plant belonging to the sunflower family (*Helianthus annuus*) which can be used for eating purposes; the *Helianthus subtuberosus*, the Indian potato which is found in the northwestern part of the prairies, or the *Helianthus tuberosus*, the Jerusalem artichoke which is widely spread across the continent.

Both these plants have thick fleshy roots, that make delightful eating.

1 medium squirrel	**2 large Jerusalem artichoke roots**
2 wild onions	**3 fingers coltsfoot salt**

Clean out the innards of the squirrel and wash it thoroughly. Scrape the skins off the Jerusalem artichokes. Wash well and cut into small cylinders. Skin the onions and chop into small pieces.

Stuff the animal with the onions, sprinkle the salt inside the cavity and add as much of the artichoke as the cavity will hold. Close the cavity by tying roots or a piece of string around the body.

Roll out a piece of clay about three-quarters of an inch thick on a flat stone and place the animal in the center. Put a large leaf across one end of the animal to divide it from the vegetables that have been placed with the animal on the sheet of clay. Cover the whole thing with another sheet of clay, making sure that all is covered without any open spots. Place the mud package in the coals of your campfire and rake coals over it. Put some wood on the coals. Let the mud pack stay in the coals for at least 2 hours. Remove the mud pack from the coals and crack it open. Take out the Jerusalem artichokes and onions and transfer to a piece of bark or a plate.

The fur and the skin of the squirrel will stay with the mud so that you can easily remove the meat and enjoy a delightful meal.

MUD BAKED STUFFED PICKEREL

2-3 pound pickerel
1 handful wild rice
1 handful bulrush shoots, finely chopped
1 handful mint, finely chopped
2 wild onions, finely chopped
2 fingers coltsfoot salt
2 fingers bear fat, or bacon fat

Clean the pickerel, leave the skin and head on, then wash in cold water. Wipe clean and rub the salt into the cavity. Mix the wild rice, bulrush shoots, mint, onions, and fat. Stuff the fish and tie together with a piece of string or a pliable root. Roll out two pieces of clay about three-quarters of an inch thick and large enough to cover the fish. Place the pickerel in the center of one of the clay cakes, place the other cake on top and seal around the edges. Rake out some coal from the fire, put the mud pack there, cover with coals and put some more wood on the fire. Cook for at least one hour. Remove the mud pack from the coals, crack open and eat directly from the mud shell.

VENISON STEAK IN A MUD PACK

2 pounds of round steak of venison
4 wild onions, thinly sliced
2 fingers coltsfoot salt
6 arrowhead tubers, thinly sliced
4 puffball mushrooms, thinly sliced

Slice the steak in one-half inch thick slices. Roll out one large piece of clay about three-quarters of an inch thick. Make sure that the clay is large enough to cover all the meat and vegetables.

Place one piece of steak in the middle of the clay sheet, next a piece of onion, then a piece of arrowhead tuber, then another piece of steak, and alternate until all the ingredients are used. Sprinkle the puffballs and salt on top and roll the clay so that all the meat and vegetables are enclosed in the clay sheet and no spot has been left open.

Rake away some of the coals and put the mud pack with the meat and vegetables in the coals. Rake some more coals on top of the mud pack. Place more wood on the fire. Cook for at least 2 hours. Remove from the coals and carefully make a hole on top of the pack. Widen the hole so that you can eat the meat and the vegetables from the mud pack, without losing any of the juices.

STUFFED GROUSE IN A MUD PACK

1 grouse	1 cup maple sap
6 wild apples or crabapples	2 fingers coltsfoot salt

Remove the innards from the grouse and wash the cavity well with cold water. Rub the cavity with salt. Cut the apples into small pieces and stuff into the cavity; then pour in the maple sap. Roll out two pieces of clay, making sure that they will cover the bird.

Place the bird in the middle of one of the clay sheets. Fold the clay as high on the bird as it will reach. Place the other clay sheets on top and fold down, making sure that the clay will overlap by at least two inches all the way around. Seal well so that no steam or juice can escape during the cooking. Place the mud pack in the coals and scrape coals on top and all around the pack. The coals must cover all of the mud pack. Place some more wood on the fire and cook for at least 2 hours. Remove the pack from the coals, break it open and eat directly from the pack.

The feathers and the skin will stick to the mud and can be conveniently removed with the mud, leaving you with a delicious meal.

PARTRIDGE STEW

2 partridges	2 fingers coltsfoot salt
4 fingers porcupine fat	4 wild onions
1 handful bulrush shoots, finely chopped	10 arrowhead tubers, sliced

Skin and draw the partridge and cut it into small serving pieces. Clean and wash the bulrush shoots and cut into small pieces. Skin and slice the wild onions. Scrape and wash the arrowhead tubers. Make a birch bark container large enough to take all the ingredients and still leave enough room to line the basket with one inch-thick mud walls and bottom. Line the basket with mud and place the container in the sun or close to the fire to partly dry.

Place the pieces of partridge, porcupine fat, bulrush shoots, onions and arrowhead tubers in the container, sprinkle the salt over the surface, cover with a large green leaf and pack some more mud on top of the leaf.

Make a hole in the coals of your camp fire, then place the basket in the hole and cover with coals and add some more wood to the fire. Keep in the fire for at least 3 hours.

Remove from the fire and cool for a few minutes. Remove the top of the mud pack and use the rest as a bowl. Serve the stew directly from the pot.

MIXED WILD GAME STEW

1 rabbit	2 fingers coltsfoot salt
1 grouse	3 fingers bacon fat
1 cup Indian vinegar	1 handful fresh mint
2 cups of water	1 finger spice bush powder
4 small wild onions, halved	

Skin and clean the rabbit and grouse. Wash well in cold water and pat dry. Cut into serving pieces and remove the bones. In a large birch bark container, mix the vinegar, water, halved onions, coltsfoot salt, mint and spice bush powder. Stir well and set aside.

Using a roasting stick, spear the pieces of meat and brown over the campfire basting with the bacon fat. When well browned, plunge the meat into the marinade and store container in a cool place: a spring fed stream, or in the snow. Make sure that the cover cannot be removed by animals. Let stand for 2 days.

Make a birch bark container which will hold all the meat and marinade. The container should be large enough so that the inside can be lined with a layer of mud or clay about three-quarters of an inch thick. Sprinkle the clay with salt and place the basket in the campfire.

After a day in the fire, the clay is hard enough to form a good pot.

Remove all the meat, spices and marinade from the container and place in the clay pot. Put the pot in the fire and simmer for about 1½ hours.

Serve the stew with roasted bulrush roots or arrowhead tubers.

MUD BAKED DUCK WITH WILD RICE STUFFING

1 medium duck
3 wild apples
3 fingers coltsfoot salt
1 handful wild rice
2 fingers fat
½ handful wild onion, finely chopped
½ handful mushrooms
2 cups maple sap
1 finger spice bush powder

Clean the duck leaving the feathers on. Pat the inside dry and rub two fingers of coltsfoot salt all over the cavity.

In a birch bark container, mix finely chopped apples, wild rice, onions, mushrooms, maple sap, remainder of the coltsfoot salt and spice bush powder. If the mixture is too wet, crumble a dried corncake and mix it into the stuffing.

Fill the cavity with the stuffing. Tie the duck together with a piece of string or a pliable root.

On a flat stone, roll out two sheets of clay, about three-quarters of an inch thick and large enough to cover the duck. Place the duck in the center of one of the clay sheets and fold the clay upwards. Place the second sheet on top of the duck and fold downwards so the clay will melt and overlap about two inches all around. Seal the clay well so that no openings are left to let steam or juices out of the mud pack.

Rake some coals out of the fire and place the mud pack in the hollow. Rake the coals over the mud pack and add more wood to the fire. Let stand in the fire for about 2½ to 3 hours.

Remove the mud pack from the coals and break open. You will find that the feathers will stick to the clay and you will have clean meat to feast on.

As you have seen, this ancient way of cooking gives you an almost unlimited variety of menus. All you need is just a little imagination and the courage to try something new and exciting.

Of the many things Mother Nature gave to Indians, tree bark was probably the most important.

The Indian used bark to construct living quarters, he made his boat of it and, last but not least, he made most of his kitchen utensils out of bark.

I have seen many utensils made from birch bark that would put modern kitchenware to shame, both in beauty and serviceability.

The Indians so dearly appreciated bark that they incorporated it into their ceremonial rites. Bark also made its imprint in their folklore.

Unfortunately the beautiful white trunks of the birch are disfigured forever when a piece of bark is removed, so only remove bark in case of an emergency, or if you can find a birch tree which has fallen.

Birch bark lasts much longer than the wood inside it, so you can remove this bark and use it for your bark utensils without damaging standing trees.

The bark is usually hard to work with and has to be prepared before it is pliable enough.

After you have removed the bark from the tree, place it tan side down on the ground and weigh it down with stones. The bark will absorb the moisture from the ground and will lend itself to be worked upon without breaking and splitting.

To make it even more pliable, soak the bark in hot water and then roll it up opposite its natural curve.

After the bark has been cured and soaked, it becomes a wonderful material for making containers.

Water and food can be boiled in birch bark containers in two different ways. First, the hot stone method can be used. That is, small stones are heated red hot and dropped into the container until the water or food boils.

The second method is to place the container directly in the coals. As amazing as it may sound, bark will not catch on fire if the level of water is higher in the bark container than the coalbed surrounding the container. How does this work?

The fluid inside the container cools the bottom and sides enough so that the bark does not burst into flames as long as the water can get in contact with the container. Remember though, that as soon as steam is formed along the sides, an insulating factor enters the picture and the flaming point of the birch bark is reached and the bark starts to burn.

I have cooked many delicious dishes in birch bark containers. Here are some of them.

BROILED BRACKEN FERN

3 handfuls bracken fern shoots   **2 fingers coltsfoot salt**

Wash and clean the bracken fern shoots well. An easy way to remove the brown rust on the fern is to rub them between your hands. Fill the birch bark container three-quarters full with water. Add the coltsfoot salt and bracken fern.

Have a good bed of hardwood coals ready and place the container in the coals. Rake coals all around the container making sure that the coals are kept well below the level of the water in the container. Remove as soon as the water boils.

Drain and serve hot with bacon fat or butter.

POPLAR PORRIDGE

2 handfuls white poplar bark   **3 cups sugar maple sap**
1 finger coltsfoot salt

Scrape the new growth found between the wood and the outer bark of the poplar. This pulp is an excellent source of vitamin C.

Place the pulp in the birch bark container and add the coltsfoot salt and maple sap. Dig a hole in the coal bed of your campfire, place the container in the hole and carefully pack some more coals around the container. Remove when the contents starts to boil. Let stand close to the fire for about 5 minutes to simmer. Sprinkle a little maple sugar over the contents and eat directly from the container.

WILD RHUBARB COMPOTE

This plant grows bountifully in the Yukon and along the Mackenzie River banks. It can grow as tall as six feet on a reddish stem.

3 handfuls of rhubarb stems, cut up into one-inch pieces	**1 piece wild ginger root** **¼ cup maple syrup**

Place the cut-up stems in a birch bark container, add two cups of water and maple syrup and place the crushed ginger root on top. Place the container in the coals and simmer for about half an hour without letting the contents boil. This makes a delightful dessert.

FISH AND WILD RICE

2 handfuls wild rice **2 fingers coltsfoot salt**	**1 pickerel skinned, boned and filleted**

Place the wild rice in the container. Add two cups of water and the coltsfoot salt. Place the container in the coals for about 35 minutes. Remove the container and add the fish. Put it back into the coals and simmer for about 15 minutes. Remove and eat directly from the container.

JELLIED SNAKE

Any one of our snakes can be used for this recipe. The rattlesnake is particularly tasty.

1 medium snake **2 cups Indian vinegar**	**1 handful mint** **2 fingers coltsfoot salt**

Skin the snake and remove the intestines. Cut into one-inch pieces. Wash in cold water. Put the vinegar, mint and the coltsfoot salt in a container; place the pieces of snake on top and cover with cold water. Let stand overnight in the marinade. Place the container in the coals in the morning and simmer slowly for 35 minutes. Remove from heat and cool. The dish is ready to eat when the jelly has set.

COYOTE OR BRUSH WOLF STEW

One hindleg of coyote **6 wild onions** **1 handful mint**	**2 large Jerusalem artichokes** **2 fingers spice bush powder** **2 fingers coltsfoot salt**

Cut the meat from the hindleg into small pieces. Wash in cold water. Fill the container with cold water about three-quarters full. Skin and quarter the onions and add to the container. Cut the mint and add. Scrape the skins from the Jerusalem artichokes and cut into small pieces and add to the container. Add the salt and the spice bush powder.

Place the container in the coals and simmer all night. The dish is then ready to be served. If you don't like vegetables cooked to a mush, wait until morning to add them, then simmer for about one hour.

As you can see, this way of cooking is about as versatile as mud baking. A great variety of dishes can be made by this method. It is a little more complicated and needs a lot of attention, otherwise the birch bark container will burst into flames.

SPIT COOKING

Undoubtedly this method is the oldest of all cooking methods and came soon after man had discovered how to make fire.

Meat can be broiled over an open fire but it is often tiresome and takes a great deal of care. A small animal such as a squirrel or rabbit can be cooked whole on a spit directly over the fire. A serious drawback with this kind of cooking is that all the juices drip into the fire and burn. But it cannot be denied that the smell of moose steaks roasting over an open fire on a cool crisp fall evening is something you must experience to believe.

Meat roasted over an open fire will improve considerably if you sear the meat in the fire before cooking it. Don't worry if the meat gets a bit black on the outside.

ROASTED RIBS

Once when I was travelling with one of my Indian guides he introduced me to a delightful meal of ribs roasted in front of the fire.

Leave the ribs together from one side of the animal. Sharpen two long sticks and work them through the ribs. Make a sauce and smear the outside of the ribs with it.

Shove the ends of the sticks into the ground in front of the fire. Baste the ribs with the sauce while they cook. When cooked on one side, lift the poles out of the ground and turn them to cook on the other side.

They can be eaten hot, but are also delicious cold.

SAUCE FOR THE RIBS

2 handfuls bear grease
¼ cup Indian vinegar
¼ handful wild mustard seeds

3 fingers coltsfoot salt
Juice from 3 wild onions
2 fingers spice bush powder

Crush the wild mustard seeds between two stones. Mix the rest of the ingredients in a kettle and place in the fire to simmer for 15 minutes, adding the mustard seeds a little at a time.

BRIGAND STEAK

A meal fit for a king can be made by cutting small cubes of deer or moose meat, slices of wild onions and slices of fat bear meat. Sharpen a green stick and alternate the deer or moose meat, onion and bear meat on the stick. Broil over the fire and serve on a hot bun of any kind.

UMU COOKING (STEAM COOKING)

This prehistoric method of preparing food was widely used by Indians all over this continent long before the white man came.

Dig a pit and line it with flat stones on the bottom and sides. Fill the pit with hardwood and light a fire. Let the fire burn for several hours or until the stones are very hot. Rake out the coals and place the food, usually wrapped in large leaves in the stone-lined hole. Fill the hole with mud and with a stick, poke a hole through the mud into the meat. Pour some water down the hole and then plug the hole. Food should be steamed for about 2 to 3 hours.

This method is excellent with food which takes a long time to cook, such as beans or bulrush roots.

To be able to really enjoy this method, I usually make myself a pot of clay and put the food in it, making the procedure much cleaner and easier to manage.

The pot is made by first making a basket out of straw, grasses or rushes. Make a long strand of grass about one inch thick. By starting at the bottom, wind the strand in tight circles, tying each strand to the next one. When the bottom is the desired size, start building the sides and continue until you reach the height you desire.

Select a good clay and line the basket. The walls and bottom should be about three-quarters of an inch thick. Place the whole thing in the sun and let it sun-dry for a couple of days.

Then place the basket with the clay in the fire and let the straw or rushes burn. Remove the clay pot and let it cool. After the pot is cool, mix a solution of silicate of calcium, potassium and aluminum. (White chalk, Kaolin and aluminum.) With a brush, smear the solution on the partly burned pottery both on the inside and outside, return it to the fire and burn it in a hot fire.

If you succeed you will have a good pot for cooking, but you may not have any luck the first time you try. I found that it was much easier to buy the solution ready-mixed from a store which handles pottery equipment.

Chapter 7

WILDERNESS COOKING:
BUCKSKIN WAYS

How often as children have we pictured outselves sitting around a campfire in the company of picturesque frontiersmen dressed in long fringed wamus and leggings, with their feet enclosed in soft soled moccasins! The name 'buckskin' was given to this kind of man because of his clothing.

The early frontiersmen were renowned as fast and confident travellers through our wilderness. To accomplish this feat, it was necessary to travel light and to depend on skill and ingenuity.

This frontier spirit is still found in many of our backwoods trappers. Many a time I have travelled in their company with a pack weighing less than five pounds and yet we were on the trail for weeks living off the land.

This is an experience I wish all youngsters had a chance to have today. But unfortunately, this breed of man is dying out, replaced by the modern trapper with snowmobile and outboard motor.

We have tried to preserve this spirit by recording here some methods and recipes on how to live well in the wilderness by taking advantage of Mother Nature's pantry.

Very seldom were cooking utensils carried in a packsack except a tin skillet which served as an all-purpose unit both for cooking and eating.

Eating tools were usually fashioned on the spot. A hunting knife was part of their gear and a fork was made by stripping a sapling of bark and sharpening one end. Plates, if needed, were made from a piece of bark.

As the buckskin was always travelling, a permanent camp kitchen was seldom set up. In his pack he carried a small amount of salt, pepper, coffee, tea and flour.

In many instances they had to travel not only soundlessly, but also smokelessly. Enemies could be tipped off by the smallest of campfires. But men had to eat to be able to function.

This is where the jerky and the pemmican came in handy. Berries and wild roots if in season were another source of smokeless food. In another part of this book we have talked about the preparation of jerky, but here are a few recipes on how to make this dish on the trail.

Jerky

Over a fire ditch, build a scaffold of poles and willows. Cover the bed with a piece of cheesecloth or an old piece of tent. Boil a big pot of water and add a lot of salt.

Cut deer or moose meat into long thin strips. Dip the meat quickly in the boiling salt water and place on top of the scaffold, making sure that the strips do not touch each other.

Build a slow smoky fire of hardwood in the fire ditch and keep it going for several days. Place the dried meat in sacks or bags for carrying on hunting or fishing trips. The meat will last a long time.

Pemmican also played an important role in the buckskin's diet. Properly made it was a tasty dish, easy to carry on the trail and it could be eaten as it was, or cooked over a campfire.

There are as many ways to make pemmican as there are trappers. Here are some recipes which are worth trying. Perhaps one of them will suit your taste buds. To start, here is *our* favorite pemmican.

Pemmican

Cut up the lean part of moose meat into long narrow strips and hang on racks to dry in the sun. Then cut it into cubes. Pound into a paste on a flat rock adding moose fat, blueberries and cranberries to taste, although the more the better. During this time, the casing from the moose innards, scraped and cleaned, has been sitting in a pot of salted water.

Stuff the casing with the paste and tie off in lengths for daily rations.

If the sun-drying method doesn't appeal to you, try this one.

Roast a moose, deer or caribou chunk over an open fire until well done. Cool and cut into small pieces, pound the meat on a flat rock and mix in a few wild onions, salt and pepper. If you have some bacon fat it is ideal, otherwise add rendered bear fat. Pound until you have a thick paste. Place the pemmican in a crock or other suitable container. Melt rendered bear fat and pour over the paste. Pemmican will keep for a long time if the container is kept in a cool place or buried in the ground about two feet deep. Each time you use some of the paste, remember to re-melt the fat and pour on top of the paste.

If it is late in the fall, here is another way to make pemmican, although this is very rich in taste.

Pound dried moose or deer meat on a clean flat rock to fine crumbs. Melt some of the moose fat and pour over the crumbs and pound again. Place the paste in birch bark or any other container that you might have with you. Set out to freeze.

Slice the paste and serve cold or fry over the campfire.

Liver and Onions

Wash the liver well in salted water. Change the water several times. Make a marinade of salted water and Indian vinegar and let it stand for half an hour with the liver in it. Drain off the marinade and pour boiling water over the liver. Pull off the membrane coating. With a sharp knife slice in quarter-inch slices. Mix flour with salt and pepper and roll liver in the flour.

Put a few strips of bacon in the frying pan and cook until crisp. Add sliced wild onions and cook until golden brown. Push the onion to one side and add the liver.

Cook the liver over medium heat for about 10 minutes per side. Serve with crisp bacon and a lot of bacon fat.

Left-Over Hash

Cut up any left-over moose or deer meat into small cubes about half-inch square. If you have any cooked arrowhead tubers, cube and set aside. Peel and cube three wild onions. Place a few strips of bacon in the frying pan and fry until crisp. Remove bacon, add the onions and cook until golden brown. Add the meat and tubers and cook for another 10 minutes or until heated right through.

Eat directly from the pan or serve on a piece of birch bark. If you have an egg, break it over the hash and sprinkle with crumbled bacon. This is a great way to start the day.

As a complement to this breakfast, have a strong cup of coffee sweetened with a piece of maple sugar.

Cornmeal Bread

If you had time to place a flat stone in the fire before you bedded down the night before, rake the stone out of the fire and clean it with a fresh evergreen bough.

Use some cornmeal from your rations and make paper-thin bread to accompany the hash.

Take three handfuls of cornmeal and a finger of salt, add enough water to make a gruel and cook until it is the same consistency as porridge. The stone should be as hot as possible; if you drop a bit of water on it the drop should sizzle away instantly.

Take some of the dough in your hand and spread it across the stone. It cooks very quickly, so you can peel it off when it starts to crinkle around the edges. Put some crushed blueberries or strawberries on top of the bread.

Baked Eggs

Have you ever eaten a baked egg? When on the trail, the buckskins and Indians often robbed a duck nest of its eggs. They tested them first, by putting them in water. If it sank, it was good to eat, but if it floated, the egg was carefully put back in the nest.

As it is against the law to rob any bird's nest, you will have to use a hen's egg.

The old timers pushed a small green stick through the egg from end to end. A quick jab against the shell will make a clean hole. If you have a piece of wire, so much the better.

Hang the egg on two forked uprights over a bed of coals. Keep turning the egg for about 10 minutes and presto, you have a baked egg. I have seen hungry trappers baking as many as eight or ten eggs on the same stick at the same time.

Baked eggs can be carried with ease on the trail, with no worry of breakage.

After a full day with paddle in hand, or travelling miles through the wilderness on foot, a simple but nourishing meal, one that was easy and quick to prepare, was required.

Supplies for the meal were often secured during the day while enroute. Food for the buckskins was a necessity, not a feast. Festive meals they looked forward to after a completed trip. The settler's wife or the Indian squaw looked after these meals for the tired travelers.

Bread, for instance, was seldom made on the trail. The closest they came to bread was bannock. This was made by putting two fingers of soda and one finger of salt in a small depression in their bag of flour. The soda and salt were mixed with some flour, and water was added a little at a time. The amount of water decided the size of the dough. It was mixed carefully to avoid lumps. When the dough was soft and could be rolled between well-floured hands, it was transferred to the frying pan. The pan was held over the fire until the bottom of the dough was baked, then the pan was propped up on its side in front of the fire to bake the top. As it cooked it rose, and turned golden brown.

But if the frying pan was busy doing other things for the meal, the dough was rolled between the hands to form a cylinder about one inch thick. It was then wrapped around a green stick in a spiral, leaving enough space between the spirals to let the heat reach all parts of the dough. The sticks were placed in front of the fire to bake. The sticks were turned from time to time to let the heat cook and brown the dough.

Chapter 8

WILDERNESS PREPARATION OF FISH

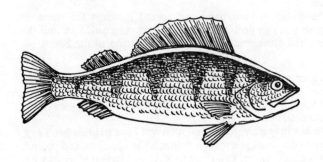

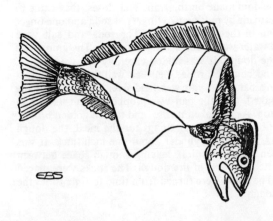

EBS

Our rivers and lakes with their bounty of fish gave an endless supply of fresh food to the tables of the early settlers and Indians.

Fish is a complete protein food similar to meat, supplying the important B vitamins and a score of minerals. Some fish also contain vitamins A and D.

To preserve the truly delicious flavor of freshly caught fish, it is vital that fish be taken care of the minute they are caught.

In the winter the problem is not so great, as fish can be frozen immediately by dipping in water to form a coating of ice which seals in the delicate flavor.

In the summer, however, it can be more of a problem as fish spoil quickly in heat or in the sun's rays.

The moment the fish is caught, slit it open with a sharp knife from the vent to the gills along the center line of the belly. Cut out the gill attachment under the throat and remove it from the head along with the entrails.

Wash the fish with cold water and wrap it in seaweed or fresh grass. Store in a box or other container in which several holes have been drilled to allow air circulation. Keep it out of the sun.

FILLETING FISH

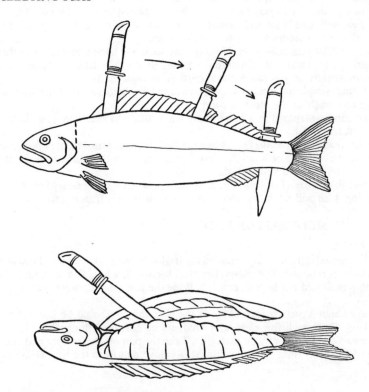

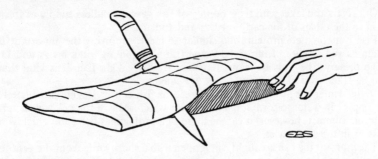

Many people like to skin and fillet fish before cooking, by this I mean removing the bones, but here is a word of advice. Don't try to fillet small fish because you will lose too much of the meat.

Perhaps the way I fillet fish is not the best way, but it is a beginning for somebody who is learning the tricks of the trade.

Place the fish on a board or a flat stone with the back towards you. Hold the fish firmly and with a sharp knife make a slit just under the head, below the gill opening and behind the fins. Run the knife along the backbone with the rib cage as a guide. Try to stay as close to the rib cage as you can by holding the free meat with one hand and carefully cut it away from the rib cage, cutting through the thin stomach skin to free the fillet.

Lay the fillet skin side down. Hold the tail with one hand and with the other cut through the meat at the fin until the knife hits the skin. Run the knife along the skin as close as you can without cutting through the skin.

It sounds simple but it takes some practice to be able to do a neat job without losing too much of the meat in the process.

Fish can be prepared in a great many ways. But whatever way you choose, don't overcook fish.

Fish is ready to put on the table when the flesh loses its translucent appearance and becomes opaque or when the flesh flakes readily with a fork, or when the flesh is easily pierced with a fork.

Never thaw frozen fish before cooking except when it is necessary for ease in handling. Fish will retain its juices when cooked from a frozen state.

COOKING METHODS FOR FISH

Pan Frying

This method is the most common on the trail or in camp. It is easy and fast and the flavor is retained. This method is ideal for small, whole fish, although the frying pan should not be too crowded. Wipe the pan clean between each batch of fish.

Have about a quarter-inch of fat in the pan; the fat should be hot but not smoking. Wipe each fish clean and dredge with seasoned flour. Put the fish in the pan and sear briefly on each side. Take the pan off the hot fire and cook about 10 minutes, more over lower heat. Remove pan from the fire. Drain off the fat.

Pan Frying Fillets or Steaks

Cut the fish into serving pieces and dip in salted milk, then flour or bread crumbs. Finely crushed corn flakes are good as a change. If you like a hard crust, dip again in the milk and flour. Sear over a hot fire on both sides in a quarter-inch of fat, move the pan to a lower heat and cook about 10 minutes per inch of thickness.

Pan Frying in Milk-Egg Mixture

Clean fish and season well with salt and pepper. Dip the fillets in a beaten egg and milk mixture. Let coating dry for about 10 minutes. Heat a quarter-inch of fat in pan and fry fish quickly on both sides allowing 4 to 5 minutes on each side for a fish fillet about half an inch thick.

Deep Fat Frying

Prepare the fish as you would for pan frying, except the dipping process is repeated to give the fish a good coating of crumbs to provide a crisp protective coat.

Melt fat in a container over the fire until a piece of bread browns evenly and fairly fast, in about 3 minutes. If you have rendered bear fat, use it. Cook the fish until it is golden brown and flaky, usually 6 to 8 minutes. Drain on a bed of evergreen boughs.

Broiled Fish

Arrange fillets or whole fish on a piece of aluminum foil. Most fish have very little fat, so brush them with butter or fat. Wrap in the foil and watch for any punctures. Wrap in large green leaves and then again in foil. Rake away some of the coals from the fire and put the package on the fire. Return the coals to the fire, put over the foil package, and cook for about 20 minutes.

Remove the package from the fire and open. Place the fish on a flat stone which you have preheated in the fire. Let the heat from the fire brown the fish.

Serve on a piece of birch bark or plate and pour the juices from the foil over the fish.

Barbecued Fish

Clean the fish and stretch it open with a couple of green sticks. Insert a sharpened stick lengthwise through the fish.

Tilt the stick over the fire and let it cook, basting it occasionally with a barbecue sauce made of a couple of tablespoons of Indian vinegar, a little fat and one tablespoon chopped wild onion or onion juice.

When the fish starts to flake, turn the stick around and cook the skin side. Be careful when removing the fish from the fire so that it will not land in the coals. Season with more barbecue sauce and serve hot.

Baked Fish

Put a piece of aluminum foil on a flat surface. Line the foil with large green leaves such as miner's lettuce or maple leaves. Lay another piece of foil on top of the leaves and put the clean fish on the foil. Fold foil over fish, put a layer of leaves on top of fold and fold bottom layer of foil over the leaves. This procedure is done to keep the fish from burning in the fire.

Cook to desired doneness depending on size and thickness of fish. Turn once.

Baked Fish in Bannock

Make a batch of bannock by mixing two handfuls of flour, two fingers of salt and four fingers of baking powder. Mix the dry ingredients well and add water until you have a soft dough. Prepare aluminum foil and leaves as above and grease the top layer of foil with fat or butter.

Put half of the dough on the greased foil. Place the clean fish on top of the dough. Sprinkle finely chopped wild onion and wild leek on top of the fish and sprinkle half a handful of powdered milk on the onions. Make a depression in the dough and pour one cup of water over the fish. Place the other half of the dough on top and make a perfect seal.

Roll up the foil, making sure that you have a watertight seal. Put the package on the coals of the campfire. Rake coals over it and cook for about 20 minutes. If you use frozen fish, halve the quantity of water and double the cooking time.

Baked Stuffed Fish

Prepare the aluminum foil as above. Place a cleaned fish on the foil with the opening side up. Chop two small wild onions finely and put in a bowl. Add two finely chopped eggs, half a handful of crushed dry bannock, two fingers of coltsfoot salt, four fingers of spice bush powder and a cup of Indian vinegar. Mix well and loosely stuff the fish with this mixture.

Roll the fish in the foil and seal. Rake some coals out of the fire, put the package in the fire and rake the coals back over the fish. Cook for about 20 minutes and eat directly from the foil.

Baked Perch Fillets

Prepare the aluminum foil as above. Grease the foil with bacon grease. In a container mix half a cup arrowhead tubers, finely cubed; a few dandelion leaves, finely chopped; two wild onions, finely chopped; two fingers coltsfoot salt, two fingers spice bush powder, one cup Indian vinegar and one cup dry bannock crumbs. Roll each perch fillet in the mixture until it is well coated. Place on the greased foil and pour the remaining mixture over the fillets. Close the foil, making sure that the foil is sealed completely. Rake some coals out of the fire, put the package in the fire and rake the coals back over the foil. Cook for about 25 minutes and serve directly from the foil.

Baked Smelts

Prepare the aluminum foil as above. Grease the foil with butter or bacon fat. Clean the smelts and cut off their heads and tails. Season each fish with coltsfoot salt and spice bush powder. Place the fish on the foil, alternating directions. Sprinkle finely crushed bannock crumbs on top.

Put more bacon grease on top of the fish and add a cup of maple sap. Close the foil, making sure that the foil is sealed completely. Sometimes it is better to make a pan shape of the foil, set the fish in it and seal. Then set that down on a larger piece of foil and seal that over the first one. Put it in the coals of the fire and cook for about 25 minutes. Serve from the foil.

Baked Mushroom-Stuffed Catfish

2 medium catfish	2 fingers fat or bacon grease
1 cup puffball mushrooms	2 fingers salt
1 wild onion, finely chopped	1 cup bannock crumbs
	1 cup Indian vinegar

Remove the head and rub the salt on the inside of the catfish. Place the fish in the center of a good sized piece of foil prepared as above. Put the bacon fat in the frying pan and heat until it is smoking. Add the mushrooms, wild onion and a little vinegar to keep the mushrooms moist. Fry until the onions are golden brown. Add the rest of the vinegar and the bannock crumbs. Set aside to cool.

When the stuffing is cool, loosely stuff the fish cavity and roll the fish up in the foil. Place the package in the coals and cook for about 30 minutes. Serve directly from the foil.

Baked Stuffed Lake Trout

1 medium lake trout	1 cup bannock crumbs
2 fingers bacon fat	1 cup wild apples, finely chopped
2 fingers salt	1 cup mint, finely chopped
2 fingers spice bush powder	Salt and spice bush powder

Prepare the aluminum foil as above and grease it well with bacon fat. Clean and wash the fish well and leave the head and tail on. Rub salt and spices in the cavity. Put a few strips of bacon in the frying pan and fry until crisp. Remove bacon and set aside. Put the apples, mint and bread crumbs in the pan and cook for a few minutes. Then crumble the bacon over the pan contents.

Loosely stuff the fish, fasten the opening with a small green sapling and loop a string around it, as you would lace shoes.

Place the stuffed fish in the middle of the foil and close it. Place in the coals of the fire to bake for 10 minutes on each side.

Remove from the fire and serve.

Boiled and Steamed Fish

Boiling fish is a simpler matter—at least that's what most people think. It's as simple as dropping fish into boiling water and cooking it for a few minutes, that is if you like a flat-tasting, nondescript mess.

If you mention court bouillon cooking to an old trapper, he won't know what you are talking about. Nevertheless, I have eaten many delightful dishes prepared in this manner, not in a fancy hotel but in a trapper's cabin hundreds of miles from the nearest city or town.

The common name for this dish in the backwoods is fish soup. But the name doesn't matter. If properly done it's a gourmet's delight.

The usual procedure is to place fish either unwrapped or in cheesecloth, in a savory liquid that has been prepared beforehand. Here is the standard bouillon I like to have on hand in camp.

2 wild onions	4 bulrush shoots, sliced
2 fingers spice bush powder	2 wild leeks
2 fingers coltsfoot salt	1 handful mint leaves
2 cups water	½ cup Indian vinegar

Place all the ingredients in a large skillet or an empty can or pot. Put in the fire to simmer for about 15 minutes. Strain off the juices through a bed of juniper branches which will add a bit of extra flavor.

Put the pot back over the fire and bring to a boil.

Cut the fish into serving pieces and drop them in the boiling juices. Simmer for about 8 to 10 minutes.

After the fish has been removed, save the bouillon to use again.

Another way to boil fish is in milk. This method was often used in the early days when fish were salted in great barrels or smoked. The milk would draw out the salt or the heavy smoke flavor and make it more palatable.

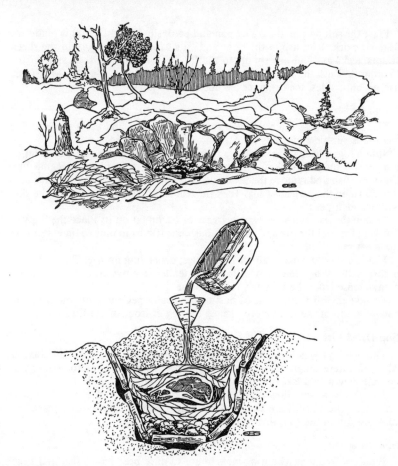

6 strips bacon	**½ handful flour**
1 wild onion	**1 cup milk**

Place the bacon in the frying pan and fry until crisp. Take out the bacon and add the onion and fry until golden brown.

Add milk, salted or smoked fish and cook for 8 to 10 minutes, depending on the thickness of the fish. Remove the fish, dissolve the flour in a little water and add this to the frying pan, stirring constantly to prevent the flour from getting lumpy. When desired thickness of gravy is obtained, add the fish again and simmer for about 5 minutes. Salt and pepper are hardly necessary as the spices are found in the milk.

Stewed Fish

4 slices fat salt pork	**4 wild leeks, finely chopped**
½ handful flour	**4 fresh bulrush shoots.**
3 wild onions	**2 fingers spice bush powder**

Place the salt pork in the frying pan and cook slowly until all fat is rendered. Remove pork. Roll fish in the flour and let sit for 10 minutes. Add the sliced onions, leeks and bulrush shoots to the fat and brown well, then simmer for 15 minutes. Push the vegetables to one side of the pan and add fish. Brown the fish on both sides, then simmer for about 10 minutes.

Planked Fish

Planking fish was often used on the trail by scouts and early settlers. The method is simple and needs little attention while cooking.

Split a log, a little larger than the spread of the fish. Rub some bacon fat or bear grease on the plank and prop it up vertically in front of the camp fire. Clean the fish and remove the head and tail. Split the fish open and place skin side down on the preheated log. Tack the fish down along the edges of the skin with wooden pegs.

Season the fish and smear some grease or bacon fat on it. Place the log vertically in front of the fire and let cook. Baste the fish from time to time; it makes the meat much juicier.

The fish should cook in about 20 minutes, depending on size. Check the fish occasionally. When the meat is flaky and tender, remove from heat before it breaks loose from the skin and falls into the fire.

To save myself the trouble of basting, I usually peg three or four strips of bacon on top of the fish before placing the log in front of the fire.

Sun Dried Fish

This method was most common in the spring when the fish run was on. More fish were caught than could be consumed, so the fish had to be prepared so that they would last through the long hot summer months.

The fish were split down the back and the backbone and the entrails were removed. The fillets were threaded on long sharpened sticks and placed on racks to dry in the sun, then packed away.

Smoked Fish

Pioneers frequently built a smokehouse to cure bear hams, fish and other foods. Indians used two methods for smoking; the open rack smokepit or the tepee arrangement, where the meat or fish hung on a rack and was exposed to the curling heat and smoke from a low but smoky fire.

There are two methods of smoking. One, the cool smoke where the fish or meat is first cured in a salt brine for days, then hung on racks in the smokehouse and smoked for days. Cold smoked meat will keep for a long time, even for years. The second method is hot smoked meat. Here, the meat is usually dipped into salt brine, hung up to partly dry in the sun, and is then put in a different kind of smokehouse, one that will produce a relatively high heat, 180 to 200 degrees for a short time. Two to three hours is usually enough time to cure the meat.

Meat smoked in this way will not keep as long as cold smoked meat. Storage time for hot smoked meat should not exceed 3 months.

A smokehouse for cold smoking is usually an elaborate building, sometimes a small log cabin, and is usually closely connected with a permanent camp or

settlement. Today more and more cold smoking is done by commercial smokers.

For the trail, the hot smoking method is the best and fastest because you don't have to spend the time building and maintaining the cool smokehouse. The hot smokehouse can simply be a piece of canvas, a few saplings, or a pair of old wooden crates placed on top of each other. The small smoky fire is maintained in the lower crate and by a series of holes to the upper box, the smoke is directed into the compartment where the meat or fish is kept.

A small tepee can also be used for concentrating the smoke. Dig a vertical trench in the side of a hill, cover the trench with saplings and evergreen boughs. On top of the evergreen cover, replace the sod that was removed for the trench.

Place the tepee over the upper outlet of the sod tunnel and make a fireplace of flat rocks in the lower end of the tunnel. Hang the meat or fish to be smoked in the tepee on saplings or wire, then light a fire in the fireplace. Cover the opening of the fireplace with a flat rock and adjust the draft by undoing some of the tarp in the top part of the tepee. Make sure that there is not too much draft, or you will burn the meat.

Avoid resinous woods such as spruce, pine, or cedar as they will blacken the food and give it a disagreeable taste.

Hardwoods such as sugar maple, hickory, alder, willow or birch are ideal fire-woods for smoking. Branches of juniper, if you can find enough, give the meat an excellent taste.

Meat cured in a mixture of maple syrup, Indian vinegar and salt results in a delightfully different taste after smoking.

Try this recipe for smoked fish on the trail.

½ cup fresh bulrush shoots
2 small wild onions
3 mint leaves

1 medium smoked fish
1 handful milk powder
1 cup water

Spread the bulrush shoots, onion slices and mint leaves in the bottom of the frying pan. Cut the smoked fish into serving pieces and arrange on top of the greens. Add a half cup of water, cover the pan and simmer for about 15 minutes. Carefully remove the fish from the pan and add the milk powder and the rest of the water. Cook for another 10 minutes. Return the fish to the pan and re-heat without boiling. Serve from the pan.

Chapter 9

BREAD BAKING: WILDERNESS WAYS

Bread, man's first manufactured food still remains his 'staff of life'. The history of the art of baking is in doubt but there is evidence of grain cultivation in about 10,000 B.C.

In the Near East there is proof of a highly developed wheat in this period.

The bread of primitive man was unleavened, flat hard sheets made by mixing pulverized grains with water. The Greeks made flat cakes over the coals and then rolled them like manuscripts.

There are many speculative ideas about the time and circumstance of the discovery of fermentation. The Egyptians are credited with the first knowledge and use of it. The leavening agent undoubtedly was wild yeast, the spores of which are found in nature.

The discovery of fermentation necessitated a change in baking methods and baking over coals was given up and ovens were constructed of clay bricks. These primitive bake ovens still can be seen in use in the Province of Quebec and in New Mexico.

The principle of the bake oven was that the hollow part of the oven was filled with firewood and the fire burned for several hours before the baking took place. The embers and the coals were raked out and the bread was baked on the floor of the oven.

In camp a primitive bake oven can easily be made by using a barrel or wooden box as a core, with a piece of hollow tree trunk as a chimney. The whole thing is then covered with about a foot of wet clay. The oven must sit in the sun for a couple of days to dry out. The hollow is then filled with firewood to burn out the wooden box.

The oven is now ready for use. If a wooden box is not available, the same effect can be achieved by building a small burrow or canopy of willow branches and covering this with evergreen boughs. This must be sturdy enough to take the weight of about a foot of wet clay. After it has dried in the sun for a few days, the branches and boughs must be burned out inside.

Never build an oven on a rock, as the rock will absorb too much heat to make a good baking floor. First build a platform of clay on which you set the oven itself. By doing it this way you have a floor which can be swept out easily before baking and this will prevent coal residue or ashes on the bread.

When Columbus came to America, he found that a staple item in the diet of the native Indians was a bread made from maize or corn.

It didn't take long for the early settlers to get used to making bread in this way until the importation of farm equipment and grain from Europe was established.

Of course at this time no bakery was to be found on this continent and baking was a highly specialized art. But it took a long time before enough land had been cleared to support the growing of wheat on a large scale. When the country started to grow westward, the trail blazers, farmers, adventurers and gold seekers had one thing in common—the sourdough starter.

The famed and legendary sourdough pot on the back of the settler's kitchen range, carried on the prospector's back and in the chuck wagon of the wagon trains was always in evidence. Wherever there was a human being, there was also a pot of sourdough.

In other words, you could almost say the sourdough kept the nation growing.

Sourdough is, according to Webster's dictionary, "Leaven, especially fermented dough saved from baking so that it can be used in the next, thus avoiding the need for fresh yeast".

Sourdough was highly prized and well taken care of in those early days. Losing it might well have meant travelling through the wilderness for many miles to the nearest settlement or trapper's cabin to get some fresh starter.

With the introduction of fresh and dehydrated yeast, the need for the sourdough starter diminished so that its use almost vanished. But today many trappers still have a pot of sourdough starter on the backs of their stoves.

A little sourdough will go a long way and last for many years if properly taken care of. Our sourdough starter is over one hundred years old and is still going strong. It was obtained from Sourdough Jack in California and originated on the Kenai Penninsula of Alaska.

With sourdough starter you can make pancakes, breads, rolls, cakes and cookies even if there is no yeast miles from camp.

Sourdough is kept alive by adding flour and warm water to the starter and letting it stand in a warm place overnight to ferment. The next morning you take out about a cup of the dough to use the next time you bake.

Sourdough doesn't have to be kept alive by occasional usage but will lie dormant for ages in the refrigerator. Of course, when you are on the trail it will be used every day. It is important to remember to save a cup each time you use it.

Many people faced with the first venture into making sourdough think it is as mysterious as the darkest part of Africa. Making and keeping sourdough is not that difficult. Granted, care must be taken; time of fermentation and temperature are important and necessary factors in making good bread.

There is no mystery in making sourdough bread; the only limitation in sourdough cookery is your imagination. But before you are well versed in this kind of cookery, it is wise to stick to recipes, and it is important that you have the right kind of material for good results. Sourdough Jack recommends that you use unbleached, white, hard winter wheat flour particularly when making breads. All-purpose flour is fine for making pancakes, cakes and cookies.

It is important to use a basic batter which is set the evening before you plan to make pancakes or bread. Take all the starter and put it in a bowl big enough to allow for expansion. The bowl should be earthenware or stainless steel, or if you are on the trail a hollow tree trunk will do just as well. Add two cups of warm water (approximately 90 degrees F.), and two and a half cups of flour. Mix thoroughly. The mixture will be thick and lumpy but it will get thinner after 10 to 12 hours in a warm spot or close to the fire. Cover the bowl with a piece of waxed paper and a linen cloth.

The first thing to do the next morning is to take out a cup of the dough *before* you add anything to the dough and put it back in the sourdough pot. This is your starter for the next batch. You are left with about four and a half cups of batter.

Sourdough Pancakes

Remaining dough	1 teaspoon salt
1 egg	1 teaspoon soda
2 tablespoons oil, or melted lard	2 tablespoons sugar
½ cup instant or evaporated milk	

Place the dough in a bowl and add egg, oil and milk. Mix well. Mix salt, soda and sugar separately and sprinkle over the dough and mix. This will leaven and cause a foaming action. Let mixture rest for about 5 minutes. Heat a griddle and grease it well.

Drop the batter by the tablespoonful on the hot griddle. Sourdough pancakes require a hotter griddle than do ordinary pancakes.

If the batter won't drop off the spoon smoothly, it wasn't warm enough during the night to produce proper fermentation. Add a little milk to the dough to get the right consistency.

Serves four.

Sourdough Blueberry Muffins

Put the starter in a bowl; add two cups of warm water and two and a half cups of flour. Mix well. Set in a warm place overnight. Remove one cup of the dough and put it back in the starter pot.

Remaining dough	1 teaspoon soda
1½ cups whole wheat flour	½ cup melted bacon grease
½ cup sugar	2 eggs
1 teaspoon salt	2 cups fresh blueberries
½ cup evaporated milk	

Mix the flour, sugar, salt and soda in a bowl. Mix eggs, bacon fat and milk and add to the remaining dough. Mix well. Add the dry ingredients with the dough and mix thoroughly. Then add the fresh blueberries.

Make separate muffin tins out of aluminum foil formed over a round piece of wood. Grease the tins and fill about three-quarters full. Place in the mud oven and bake for about 30 to 35 minutes. If you don't have a mud oven, a reflector oven made from a tin can will do.

Sourdough Golden Honey Bread

This recipe was given to me by an old sourdough up in Alaska. I have never had bread so light and golden.

Put the starter in a bowl, add two cups warm water and two cups whole wheat flour. Let stand overnight in a warm place. Take away one cup of the dough and put it back in the sourdough pot. To the remainder of the dough add:

4 cups whole wheat flour	¼ cup sugar
2 cups milk	2 teaspoons salt
2 tablespoons butter or bacon fat	2 teaspoons soda
½ cup wild honey	

Scald the milk and melt the fat and the honey in the milk. Allow to cool to lukewarm. Mix the sugar, salt and soda. Blend the basic dough, milk mixture and two cups of flour together. Sprinkle the dry mixture on top of the dough and stir gently. Set dough in a warm place covered with a cloth for 30 minutes.

Break down and sift in the remaining two cups of flour until the dough is too stiff to stir with a spoon.

Turn out on a floured board and start to knead with your hands, adding enough wheat flour to keep the dough smooth and firm. Knead until light and satiny. Break the dough down into sections or flatten it out into round cakes. Grease the tops and set in a warm spot. Let it double in bulk again.

Bake in a moderate oven, 325 degrees F. until it sounds hollow when thumped on top, about one hour.

Remove from the oven and turn out on a floured towel. Butter the top crusts.

Sourdough Pinch-Offs

This is for a quick bread. Traditionally the dough was pinched off and baked in a Dutch oven.

½ cup sourdough starter	2 tablespoons honey
1 cup of milk	¾ teaspoon salt
2½ cups whole wheat flour	1 teaspoon baking powder
½ teaspoon soda	Bacon fat

Mix the starter, milk and one cup of the flour in a large bowl. Let stand overnight in a warm place to rise.

In the morning, turn this very soft dough out on one cup of flour on a board. Melt the honey in a little warm water and add to the dough. Combine the soda, salt and baking powder with the remaining one-half cup of flour. Sprinkle it over the dough and the baking board. Work the dry ingredients into the dough with your hands, kneading lightly. Roll out to one-half inch thickness. Cut out the biscuits with a cutter and dip each in bacon fat. Place either in a Dutch oven or close together in a square pan and set in a warm place to rise for about half an hour.

Bake in a moderately warm oven, 375 degrees F. for about 30 minutes.

Sourdough Corn Bannock

This recipe was given to me by an old trapper on the trail one cold morning while we were in the Rockies hunting grizzly bear. "If the grizzly don't come to taste this bannock, he is gone for good", said the old man as he walked over to his bedroll to get his sourdough starter. Believe it or not, the old man had been sleeping with the sourdough starter in his sleeping bag to keep it warm.

1½ cups uncooked yellow cornmeal	1 cup sourdough starter
1¾ cups evaporated milk, diluted	¼ cup bacon fat
2 eggs	¾ teaspoon salt
3 tablespoons sugar	¾ teaspoon soda

Combine cornmeal and milk in a bowl. Add the eggs, sugar and starter. Mix thoroughly by beating the ingredients. Add the melted bacon fat, salt and soda, stirring until blended.

Place your frying pan in the fire and melt to grease the pan. Spoon the dough into the frying pan. Put the pan over the fire and cook for 5 minutes. Then prop the pan vertically in front of the fire and bake until done, about 15 to 20 minutes or until a wood sliver can be inserted in the middle and come out clean.

Fresh Fruit Sourdough Breakfast Rolls

¾ cup sourdough starter	½ teaspoon soda
1 cup evaporated milk	1½ teaspoons salt
4 cups whole wheat flour	4 tablespoons bacon fat
½ cup honey	¼ cup brown sugar
1 egg	1 teaspoon cinnamon
1 teaspoon baking powder	1 cup blueberries

While visiting a trapper friend in Northern Ontario in the late summer, I was served these sourdough rolls for breakfast. As the fishing hadn't been too good, we passed the time picking blueberries which were just ripe.

Mix the milk and two cups of the flour in a bowl. Cover and let stand at the back of the stove or warm place overnight. The next morning, melt the honey and bacon fat, cool, then mix in the egg and beat until frothy. Add this to the sourdough. Sift together the remaining flour, soda, baking powder and salt. Sprinkle over the basic dough and mix thoroughly.

Turn out on a floured bread board and knead until the dough is smooth and velvety. Don't add more flour than just enough to keep the dough from sticking to the board.

Roll dough into a rectangle shape approximately sixteen by eight inches. Mix the brown sugar and the cinnamon. Sprinkle over the dough.

Spread the blueberries evenly over the dough and roll, starting from the long side of the dough. Cut into nine rolls.

Brush the bottoms and tops with a little melted butter and place in a square pan. Cover the pan with a towel and let rise in a warm place until double in size. Bake in a medium oven, 375 degrees F. for about 35 to 40 minutes.

Sourdough Rye Bread

Add to the sourdough starter, two cups of whole wheat flour and two and a half cups of warm water. Let it stand overnight in a warm, draft-free place. The next morning, use all of the sourdogh except one cup which goes back into the sourdough pot.

Basic sourdough starter	1 teaspoon anise seeds
¼ cup brown sugar	1 tablespoon bacon fat
¼ cup honey	1 teaspoon salt
1½ teaspoons caraway seeds	2 cups rye flour

Heat together in a little water, sugar, honey, spices and bacon fat. Cool to lukewarm. Add the mixture to the sourdough and beat well, adding the rye flour during the beating of the dough.

Turn out on a floured board and knead until the dough is smooth and satiny. Place the dough in a greased bowl, cover with waxed paper and a towel. Let rise until it doubles in size which takes about 2 to 4 hours.

Knead and shape into loaves or round cakes. Place on cookie sheets, brush with melted shortening or sugar water. Keep in a warm draft-free place and let rise until doubled.

Bake in a moderate oven, 375 degrees F. for an hour.

Sourdough is very versatile and can be used in many ways, such as sweet quick breads, cakes and cookies.

As you can imagine, a lot of experimenting was done in the field of baking in the early days. Unfortunately, most of these recipes were forgotten when yeast was made readily available. But even today, many old settlers and farmers are still raising bread from a sourdough starter.

We have tried to save all the recipes we have found during our travels in the backwoods. But we are sure that many thousands more are still hidden in long-forgotten home libraries. For anyone who might have access to old bread recipes, but who doesn't have a starter, here is the way to begin:

2 cups flour	1 package dry granulated yeast
2 cups warm water	1 yeast cake

In a bowl, mix the ingredients well and put the bowl in a warm place or in the oven overnight with the heat as low as possible. The next morning, the dough should be bubbly or frothy. Some people call it sponge or spoke yeast.

Take out a cup of starter, put it in a scalded pint sealer with a tight cover and store in the refrigerator for future baking.

Sourdough Oatmeal Cookies

When travelling in the northern part of Canada, one is often surprised at the variety of delicious cookies and cakes made from sourdough starter. City people who have never had the experience of eating these delights doubt that the sour-smelling starter can produce sweet tasting cookies and cakes. Try this recipe if you have to be convinced.

1½ cups honey or wild honey	½ teaspoon cloves
1 cup shortening or bacon fat	2 teaspoons spice bush powder
2 cups thick sourdough batter	1 teaspoon baking soda
3 cups rolled oats	2 cups whole wheat flour
1 teaspoon cinnamon	

Mix honey and shortening well. Add the sourdough and rolled oats. Mix the dry ingredients together, sprinkle on top of the batter and mix well with your fingers. Place the bowl in the refrigerator for an hour. Roll out the dough on a floured board and cut with a cookie cutter. Place cookies on a greased cookie sheet and bake for about 15 minutes in a moderate oven, 375 degrees F.

Cool and serve, or, if you want to make a double cookie, use cooked dates or strawberry jam as a filling.

Sourdough Doughnuts

This recipe was given to me in a small Norwegian settlement in northwestern Ontario by Mrs. Oscar Berg. She claimed that by using her method for making doughnuts, you couldn't go wrong and we have to agree, as we have never had a failure.

2 cups white wheat flour	1 egg
1 teaspoon baking powder	½ cup sugar
½ teaspoon salt	1 cup sourdough starter
½ teaspoon soda	½ cup milk
1 teaspoon cinnamon	2 teaspoons oil

Sift the first five ingredients together. Beat the egg and sugar together and stir in the sourdough, then add the milk and oil. Add the sifted ingredients to the dough. Knead on a floured board to a fairly stiff dough. Roll it out to one-half inch thickness and cut out with a cookie cutter.

Place the doughnuts on a greased cookie sheet. Cover and let rise in a warm oven for one hour. Lift them carefully off the sheet with a spatula and drop them into deep fat heated to about 370 degrees F. Fry to a rich golden brown.

Drain on absorbent paper. Roll in a mixture of sugar and cinnamon, if desired.

Sourdough Chocolate Cake

Sitting in Trapper Sven's cabin and watching the big Swede with hands the size of dinner plates, no one would think he could handle as delicate an instrument as an egg beater without crushing it to a mass of bent wires and broken gears. But when he began to make a cake, a recipe handed down from his mother, he was as precise as a surgeon. After tasting his masterpiece we wondered why this man was living in the wilderness when he could have been a chef in a four star restaurant. Here is the recipe he gave us.

½ cup sourdough starter	½ teaspoon salt
1 cup water	1 teaspoon vanilla
1½ cups flour	1 teaspoon cinnamon
½ cup evaporated milk	2 teaspoons soda
1 cup of sugar	2 eggs
½ cup shortening	3 squares semi-sweet chocolate

In a bowl, mix the sourdough starter with the water, flour and milk. Mix well and place in a warm spot for about 3 hours.

Cream the sugar, shortening, salt, vanilla, cinnamon and soda in a bowl. Add the eggs one at a time and beat the mixture well. Combine the creamed mixture and the melted chocolate with the sourdough and fold together, making sure all is well blended.

Pour the batter into one nine inch-square pan and bake at 350 degrees F. for about 30 minutes. Remove from oven and cool upside down on a plate.

Hardtack — Flat Bread

Hardtack or flat bread was often favored by the early settlers and scouts because it was easy to carry on long trips in the wilderness and at the same time was almost weightless.

The dried round cakes of hardtack could be carried for months on end without getting stale. Also, the whole rye bread was nourishing.

Hardtack could be used as a complement to any food where soft bread was normally used. Or, it could be softened in water and boiled to make a palatable porridge mixed with wild berries. Served with milk in a bowl, this was an easy dish to prepare in the wilderness. Another method was to crumble it in a bowl, add a handful of cranberries, a little sugar and milk.

Rye Hardtack

This recipe is taken from a 150 year-old handwritten cookbook and it makes delightful bread. It is good in flavor, nourishing, and light for the traveller to carry.

2 cups graham flour	1 cup lard, melted
2 teaspoons salt	2 cups buttermilk
1 teaspoon soda	White flour

In a large mixing bowl, blend the graham flour, salt and soda. Add the boiling hot lard to the mixture and stir well. Add the buttermilk which should be at room temperature.

Knead the dough in enough flour to make it hard enough to roll paper thin. Place on top of the stove to cook, or use a heavy pancake grill. Each piece should be a ten inch circle with a center hole.

The bread will bake in a very short time. Remove it from the stove and hang it on long rods in the pantry to dry completely.

Flat Bread

This recipe comes from the same cookbook as the one above and some ingredients have been changed slightly to meet modern standards.

1½ cups bleached whole wheat flour	½ cup graham flour
¼ teaspoon salt	⅛ cup lard
¼ teaspoon soda	¼ cup whipping cream
2 tablespoons sugar (optional)	¼ cup buttermilk

Sift the flour, salt, soda and sugar together three times. Add the graham flour and cut in the lard as you would for a pie crust. Add the cream and the buttermilk. Knead out on a floured pastry board using just enough flour to prevent sticking.

Divide the dough into eight parts and let it rest for at least 15 minutes. Roll out the dough on a floured board very thinly. Cut in six to eight inch squares, then prick with a fork. Bake on racks in a preheated oven set at 350 degrees F. for 15 minutes.

Remove from the oven and cool on racks. Store in a cool dry place. This bread will last for months without getting moldy.

QUICK BAKING ON THE TRAIL

When on the trail you usually haven't much time for baking. But nevertheless it's good to have some sort of bread to accompany meat or stew.

Since early man started to prepare food, food and its preparation have been fascinating subjects to hordes of hungry people, and cooking over the campfire is magic to us even today.

Today's man has lost one of the most important features of cooking because our completely enclosed bake ovens and stoves take away the aroma of cooking. On the trail one looks forward to the summons "come and get it" after nostrils have been tickled with heavenly smells coming from the campfire.

What smells better than freshly made bread? It may not be the white, store-bought loaf you are used to, and it may even be black from the coals it has been baked over, but the aroma is still the same.

The camp cook usually doesn't have the measuring tools which are found in modern kitchens, so he has to improvise with materials on hand.

A "handful" is the quantity of dry material that you can scoop up in your hand, filling it as full as you can.

For baking powder, salt or spices the fingers are used. Use as many fingers as are called for in the recipes by holding them together and dipping them in the material, lifting out as much as you can with the fingers and thumb without turning the hand.

For fat and grease use your little finger as a scoop. Often the camp cook uses an old trick for mixing the different ingredients by using his bag of flour for mixing the dough.

Make a hole in the middle of the flour and then add the baking powder, salt and water and work at it in the top of your flour bag. Only as much flour will adhere to the dough as you want. Mix until the dough is of such consistency that you can roll it between your well-floured hands.

TWIST

The twist is the most common biscuit you are served on the trail. To make biscuit dough, take a handful of flour for each twist you are going to make. Add two fingers of salt and three fingers of baking powder. Add one finger of lard or bacon fat.

Mix the dry ingredients first on a piece of bark, then work in the lard or bacon fat. Make a hollow in the mixture and add water or milk until you have a stiff dough.

Flour your hands and shape the dough into long strings about three-quarters of an inch thick and twelve inches long. Prepare short pieces of green saplings about one inch in diameter, by removing the green bark.

The long string of dough is wound around the saplings leaving enough space between the spirals so that heat can reach around the dough, and also to give the dough enough space to rise.

Place the sticks close to the coals of your campfire and let cook, turning the sticks occasionally to bake the dough evenly. If you have a reflector-oven, the dough can be made into biscuits with the oven placed in front of the fire, at a distance so that it is not too hot or too cold. An old trick to find this distance is to hold your hand in front of the oven for 3 to 4 minutes without burning yourself.

ASH BREADS

Our early settlers made bread without pots or pans. The only thing they needed for baking was a good hardwood fire. Build this hardwood fire on a flat rock at least one-half hour before you intend to use it, so when you are ready to bake the bread you will have a good bed of hardwood coals and the rock will be well heated.

When ready to bake, brush away any embers on top of the flat rock, and place the bread well floured on the hot rock. Then cover the bread with hot ashes and top with red hot coals.

Test the bread from time to time with a straw or a wood sliver. When dough no longer adheres to the straw, the bread is ready. Brush away ashes and coals and remove the bread. Brush off the ashes from the bread and use it as is.

My favorite recipe was given to me by an outstanding chuck-wagon chef in southern Texas, and here it is.

2½ cups flour	2 teaspoons baking powder
¼ cup skim milk powder	¾ cup water
2 tablespoons egg powder	1 tablespoon melted bacon fat
½ teaspoon salt	

Mix the flour, milk powder, egg powder, salt, baking powder in a bowl. Sift through a coarse sifter three times and return to the bowl. Add the water and the melted bacon fat and mix well with a spoon. Shape into mounds, brush with more bacon fat and roll in flour. Place on the hot stone and proceed as above.

The greasing and rolling in flour will give you a hard crusted bun when baked.

Ash bread baking is a simple but enjoyable way to make bread in the bush or on the trail.

If berries are in season, don't be afraid to use a lot of them in the dough. If you have raisins with you use them also.

TO MAKE AND USE WILDWOOD FLOUR

Indians often used substitute flour for the maize that normally was produced from corn. They obtained this from cattail or bulrush roots.

Making flour out of the roots of the cattail and the bulrush takes a lot of time and energy. But don't let this discourage you, because in an emergency situation it may be necessary to resort to this century-old Indian method. There are two methods which can be employed. First, the slow and time consuming one.

Clean the roots thoroughly and then dry them well by the fireside or in the sun (sun drying takes longer — sometimes weeks). Remove all the long fibers from the dried product and pound the dry pulp to a flour. The texture of the flour depends on how much energy you expend on the pounding.

The end result of this process is sweet in taste and not unlike that of musty wheat.

This flour can be used for making cakes or pies and is excellent for pancakes and flapjacks.

A faster method, is to pull up the roots of the bulrush or the cattail, clean, scrape, slice into small pieces, remove the fibers, add a little water and boil into a thick gruel. Place the gruel in large shallow pans or bowls in the sun or close to the fire. Let all the water evaporate.

When the gruel is bone dry, place it on a flat rock and by using another rock, pound the dried gruel to a fine flour. The quality of the flour depends on how much time and effort is given to the pounding. The more you pound the finer the flour.

BULRUSH FLOUR PANCAKES

We had been camping along the Mackenzie River for two weeks — Indian Joe and myself. The fishing was tremendous so our stay had been longer than anticipated. Our grub stake was low on bacon and flour, but we were reluctant to go out of the wilderness as this meant a three-day trip by canoe.

Joe had suggested that we make some flour, and as I was interested in how it was done, I agreed to get the bulrush roots. Bulrushes were growing plentifully along the river-banks so that I started there. I wasn't too successful

until Joe come along and told me that I would find the job easier downriver where the river had overflowed its banks in the spring and made a delta marsh.

Here I could collect the roots without getting wet. When I had a burlap bag full, I returned to camp where we cleaned and boiled the roots.

One morning a few days later, I was awakened by the aroma of freshly made pancakes. Here is the recipe Joe used that morning.

2 cups bulrush flour
3 teaspoons baking powder
2 tablespoons sugar
¾ teaspoon salt

1 tablespoon egg powder
1¼ cups condensed milk
3 tablespoons margarine

He mixed the dry ingredients in a frying pan. Then he added the melted margarine and milk to the flour mixture.

He worked the dough as little as possible until the mixture just held together, then he placed the frying pan in the campfire and let it stand there over medium heat for 15 minutes and, presto, we had one large pancake.

We used the rest of the flour for the two-week duration of our fishing trip, and he made many other goodies with the bulrush flour we had produced.

BULRUSH CRANBERRY MUFFINS

1 cup cranberries	¼ cup sugar
½ cup sugar	1 egg, or equal amount egg
2 cups bulrush flour	powder
3 tablespoons baking powder	1 cup condensed milk
1 teaspoon salt	4 tablespoons margarine

Mix the cranberries with the half cup of sugar in a bowl and let stand while preparing the muffin mixture.

Beat the egg powder and milk together in the frying pan. Mix the bulrush flour, baking powder, salt and one-quarter cup of sugar on a piece of bark. Make sure that the dry ingredients are well mixed. Add the melted margarine to the egg-milk mixture, then add the dry ingredients and mix well. Mix only until the dry ingredients are moist. Add the cranberries to the mixture. Make muffin tins out of pieces of aluminum foil by folding the foil over a rounded piece of wood.

Fill the muffin tins three-quarters full and bake in a reflector oven or, by placing the muffin tins tightly in the frying pan and propping the pan in front of the fire.

The muffins are ready when a wood sliver inserted in the middle comes out dry.

They are delicious split in half and smeared with margarine which has been slightly salted, or with butter.

BULRUSH BLUEBERRY BUCKLE

Indian Joe gives the credit for this recipe to an old trapper and his Indian wife living in the remote wilderness of the Mackenzie River.

½ cup sugar	*Topping:*
2 cups bulrush flour	½ cup sugar
2½ teaspoons baking powder	½ cup bulrush flour
¼ teaspoon salt	½ cup butter or margarine
1 egg or equal amount egg powder	½ cup powdered wild ginger
1 cup condensed milk	
1 pint blueberries	
¼ cup bacon fat	

Mix the sugar, bulrush flour, baking powder and salt in a bowl. Make sure that all the ingredients are well mixed. Beat the egg or egg powder with the milk and melted bacon fat. Make a well in the dry flour mixture and add the egg and milk mixture all at once. Stir quickly until all the dry ingredients are just moistened. Pour the mixture into the frying pan and cover with blueberries.

Mix the sugar, flour and wild ginger well, and sprinkle on top of the blueberries. Cut the butter or margarine into small pieces and dab on top of the dry topping.

Place the frying pan in a reflector oven and bake for at least one hour. If you don't have a reflector oven, cover the frying pan with aluminum foil. Place on a preheated flat stone, cover with ashes and glowing coals and bake for about the same time.

Remove from the coals, making sure that all the ashes are well dusted off before removing the foil.

Chapter 10

CORN

Corn is a member of the grass family (Gramineae) and is known by the scientific name of *Zea mays*.

It is widely accepted that the use of corn originated in Central America. There are several opinions on the subject, but it has been established that North American Indians used corn long before America was discovered.

Indian corn, also called maize, has large roundish compressed parallel rows of fruit. The parallel-veined long leaves were often used as fodder or as foil to wrap up food before it was placed in the coals for cooking.

Most of today's corn cookery comes from Mexico or New Mexico where they still use the corn cooking methods of the early days. Corn cookery can be fascinating, but it takes time as well as patience.

Guisar, a word often used by the Mexican homemaker has no direct translation into English but roughly means to dress up food, perhaps only by adding onions or a spice. Good food deserves this care to prevent it from tasting flat.

We feel that corn has been so important to our heritage that we have devoted a chapter to it.

Ash Cakes

Here is perhaps the oldest corn dish in existence. This recipe probably goes back to prehistoric times and the method is very simple.

Mix half a teaspoon of salt with one cup of corn meal and add hot water until the swollen corn meal can be worked into a ball. The ball is then buried in the hot ashes of the campfire and baked until cooked, usually about 15 to 20 minutes. Rake it out of the ashes, brush clean and it's ready to eat.

A simple way to make Johnny Cake is to mix half a teaspoon salt with one cup of corn meal and add just enough water to form a ball of dough. Flatten the ball to form a pancake about one inch thick and fry in sizzling hot melted grease in the frying pan.

Tortillas

The first time I had native-made tortillas was on the trail in New Mexico cooked by my Hopi Indian guide. The tortilla not only complemented the frijoles (beans) but we used it as a spoon to scoop up the beans.

Tortillas are wafer-thin corn meal cakes. They can also be made of wheat, but freshly ground corn meal makes a better tasting cake. Here are both recipes.

Cornmeal Tortillas

Take two cups of finely ground corn meal, add one teaspoon of salt and some warm water. Mix the ingredients into a stiff dough and set aside for 20 minutes. If you have trouble getting the dough to stick together, add a little white flour.

Wet your hands, separate the dough into small balls about the size of eggs and pat them into thin pancakes. Bake in a lightly greased frying pan and brown on both sides.

Wheat Tortillas

To two cups of wheat flour, one teaspoon of salt, one and a half teaspoons of baking powder, work in about one tablespoon of fat and cold water until you have a stiff dough. Knead on a floured board. Make small balls about the size of eggs, then flatten the balls into paper-thin wafers and bake on a greased griddle or in a frying pan.

Travelling Indians often carried with them a bag of corn kernels as emergency food.

To prepare this kind of food, strip the kernels from the cob and parch them in a frying pan. Make sure that they don't scorch. Pound or grind between two stones into a fine meal, just fine enough to be drinkable when mixed with water.

Two heaping tablespoons of this flour mixed with one-half cup of honey and a cup of warm water will give you a substantial meal on the trail.

True Indian corn meal was white and soft and was produced from the Tuscarora corn. The meal from this corn was white and floury, altogether different from today's corn meal which is granulated and yellow.

Many Indian tribes leached their corn in a weak solution made of birch ashes and boiling water. The corn was boiled in this solution until the outer covering of the kernel loosened. Then the corn was washed thoroughly in cool water and the hull was removed.

The half cooked corn was then ready to be pounded into a white, soft meal which was used for baking and for many other uses which réquired meal.

A delightful breakfast dish can be made by preparing corn kernels and pounding them to a paste. Line a large kettle with big leaves several layers deep and fill with the corn paste and maple syrup. Smooth the top of the paste and place several layers of leaves on top. Cover the leaves with white hardwood ashes and then heap on glowing coals.

Put the kettle in thè remaining coals and let cook overnight. Sometimes the top leaves have to be changed and fresh ashes and coals added to the top of the kettle.

There are several different names for this dish among the Indians but the best known is the one the Seneca Indians have given it, "O-gon-sah".

Corn Bread

Chief Kit-Pou once told me how his mother used to bake corn bread on top of the stove when he was a child.

1 cup whole wheat flour	1½ cups corn meal
2 teaspoons baking powder	1 egg, beaten
3 tablespoons sugar	1 cup milk
1 teaspoon salt	½ cup bacon grease

Mix the egg, milk and melted bacon fat in a bowl and let stand for 5 minutes. Sift the flour, baking powder, sugar and salt over the egg mixture and fold in the corn meal. Stir until all ingredients are moist and well mixed. Pour into a hot, well greased frying pan, cover tightly and bake on top of the stove over low heat for at least half an hour.

Remove from the stove and turn upside down on a rack, leaving the frying pan as a cover until cold. Cut into squares and then split in half. Serve with honey between the layers.

Here is our version of the same bread and the way we like to make it when we are established in camp:

2 tablespoons egg powder	¼ cup melted bacon fat
6 tablespoons water	3 teaspoons baking powder
1 cup milk	1 teaspoon salt
½ cup honey	2 cups corn meal

Mix the egg powder and the water, set aside and let stand for at least one hour. Scald the milk and add the honey and bacon fat. When cold add the egg mixture. Put the corn meal into a bowl and sift the baking powder and the salt over it. Mix thoroughly and add the liquid with constant stirring, making sure that all the ingredients are moist.

Put the batter into a well-greased eight inch-square cake pan. Bake in a 400 degree F. oven for about 40 minutes. Remove from the oven and cool on a cake rack. If berries are in season, split the cake in two layers and put crushed berries between the layers.

Flour Gruel

The New Mexico Indians often carried toasted flour with them on the trail. Flour treated this way can be carried for a long time without getting sticky if the weather is hot or damp. To make a tasty gruel, use it as follows.

2 tablespoons flour, toasted	1 teaspoon salt
2 tablespoons honey	½ teaspoon anise seed
1 cup boiled water	

Dissolve the honey in boiling water, mix the flour in a little water and add to the honey. Stir until it thickens and add the salt and anise seed. Pour in a bowl and add diluted condensed milk if desired.

Corn Fritters

I remember a cold crisp morning in a small shanty in the northern part of Alberta when I was awakened by the mouth-watering aroma of hot corn. My Indian guide, Smoky Bear, a Cree with many years of experience in the wilderness, was making breakfast for us. Here is the recipe for his corn fritters.

2 tablespoons egg powder	½ teaspoon sugar
6 tablespoons water	1 tablespoon wild onion, minced
1½ cups cooked corn kernels	½ cup wheat flour
½ teaspoon salt	1 cup bacon fat
¼ teaspoon pepper	

Mix the egg powder in the water and let stand for about half an hour. Then stir in the corn, salt, pepper and sugar. Mix well without over-mixing. Melt the bacon fat in the frying pan and heat until it starts to smoke. Drop the batter in with a spoon, spacing the batter to avoid crowding.

Fry until the underside is brown, then turn and brown the other side. Drain fritters by placing them on freshly cut evergreen boughs and serve with honey and freshly cooked crisp bacon.

Juniper Smoked Corn

We were busy smoking meat from a freshly killed moose when the old trapper I was visiting told me to get some corn from his corn field. I gathered several cobs and he put them in boiling water to loosen the kernels from the cobs. After scraping the kernels off the cobs, he placed them on a screened frame and set them in the smokehouse with the meat.

The next day he served smoked corn with smoked moose tongue. Here is the way he prepared the corn after smoking.

3 tablespoons butter	¼ teaspoon pepper
1½ cup smoked corn kernels	4 tablespoons condensed milk
½ teaspoon salt	

Melt the butter over low heat in a frying pan. Stir in the corn and braise for about 5 minutes, shaking the pan all the time. Stir in the salt, pepper and milk. Continue stirring for about 10 minutes until the mixture thickens.

Serve with any smoked meat or fish.

Scalloped Red Pepper and Corn

This dish is a favorite among the Hopi Indians in New Mexico.

4 cups white corn kernels	1 teaspoon salt
2 red peppers, finely chopped	½ teaspoon dry mustard
1 can cream of celery soup	1½ cups seasoned bread stuffing
½ cup evaporated milk	½ cup melted butter

Place the corn and red pepper in a small pot. Add the soup, milk, salt and mustard and stir over low heat. Melt the butter and mix into bread stuffing. Line the bottom of a nine by six inch baking dish with half the stuffing, pour the corn mixture over the stuffing and cover the corn with the remaining stuffing.

Bake in a 375 degree F. oven for about 30 minutes.

Serve with pork chops or fried ham.

Chili Corn

This is a quick way to prepare corn on the trail.

1 14-ounce can kernel corn	2 tablespoons mint, finely
¼ cup sour cream	chopped
	1 teaspoon chili powder

Drain the corn and mix the corn with the sour cream in a small pot. Add the mint and the chili powder and heat thoroughly without bringing to a boil. The dish should be ready to serve in about 10 minutes.

Aunt Thelma's Corn Chowder

On many homesteads in the backwoods, corn is an essential staple and has to do many things for the cook. While visiting an old trapper and his wife, I was served a chowder which was one of the best I have ever tasted. The recipe is simple but the result is delicious.

4 slices salt pork, diced	2 cups fresh corn kernels
½ cup wild onion, diced	4 tablespoons wheat flour

1 cup arrowhead tubers, peeled   ½ cup cold water
2½ cups chicken broth   1 pint hot milk

Fry salt pork slowly in a deep frying pan until it is crisp. Add the onions and cook until golden brown. Add the tubers and chicken broth. Cover and simmer for about 20 minutes. Add the fresh corn and simmer for another 15 minutes.

Mix the flour with water and stir until it becomes a smooth paste. Add to the frying pan and bring to a boil, stirring constantly. Stir in the milk and re-heat without boiling. Add seasoning if necessary.

Baked Corn

On the trail or in camp, corn on the cob can be baked easily and with little effort. Just break off the silk tassels and twist the husks tightly around that end. Scoop out a shallow hole in the ground and build a good hardwood fire in the hole.

When the fire has burned down, rake out the coals and put the corn in the hole. Cover with ashes and heap coals on top. Cooking time will depend on the freshness of the corn.

Corn and Moose Meat Casserole

Here is a quick and easy way to prepare a casserole on a camping trip if you have a Coleman oven or a mud oven at your disposal.

2 cups fresh corn kernels   ¼ pound moose meat, smoked
      or   and finely chopped
1 14-ounce can corn, Mexican style   1 can tomato soup
2 tablespoons wild onion, chopped   2 cups potatoes, sliced
1 can cream of celery soup

Place the corn in a saucepan and simmer for about 15 minutes. Stir in the onion, celery soup, tomato soup and the cubed moose meat and simmer for another 15 minutes. Grease a six by nine inch casserole and spread the mixture over the bottom and cover with the sliced potatoes. Cover the top with aluminum foil and put in a 350 degree F. oven for about 45 minutes. If you wish, sprinkle the potatoes with breadcrumbs, grated cheese or add dots of butter.

Corn Bread with Sausages

I was first introduced to this dish in our hunt camp many years ago.

3 cups of corn meal flour   ½ cup water
½ teaspoon salt   1½ cups applesauce
1 teaspoon baking powder   1 pound brown-and-serve
2 tablespoons bacon fat   sausages

Combine the corn, flour, salt and baking powder in a bowl. Make a well in the middle of the flour and add the water and melted bacon fat. Knead the dough until it is soft and pliable but rather loose. Spread the applesauce in a well-greased eight inch baking dish. Put the dough on top of the applesauce. Arrange the sausages on the dough and put in a preheated oven at 400 degrees F. for 20 minutes.

Remove from the oven, turn upside down and serve. As a topping for individual servings, try maple syrup.

Roasted Corn

We have left this method of preparing corn to the last because it is the easiest, although not the best way. We do not particularly like the taste of roasted corn, but it may well pass in an emergency.

To prepare the corn for roasting, cut the ear at the butt so that the core of the cob is revealed. A sharp stick is inserted securely into the butt. The husks are left on because they protect the corn from being burned when the cob is held over the fire. Keep turning the ear over hardwood coals until the corn is ready to eat.

Chapter 11

WILDERNESS BEVERAGES

After a certain length of time in the wilderness, the craving for any kind of beverage other than water soon gets the upper hand.

The early settlers soon learned to take advantage of Mother Nature's richly stocked pantry, and the Indians had for generations utilized many fruits, berries and roots to make palatable drinks.

The favorite drink in the north woods is tea, followed by strong brewed coffee. Not surprisingly, the tea and coffee you carry are the first of your supplies to run out.

But if you know wild plants, substitutes can easily be made with plants that are probably growing all around you. We would like to mention the most common plants which can be used to great advantage by the woodsman on lengthy wilderness trips or on trips where packing has to be kept to a bare minimum.

Dandelion Coffee

A strong coffee can be made out of the roots of this common plant. Collect the roots, wash and scrape them well. Put them on a piece of aluminum foil and let them dry in front of the campfire. When the roots have turned almost black and are well dried, cut them into small pieces and grind between two stones.

The dried roots can either be mixed with the coffee you have, or used as coffee, one teaspoon for each cup.

Corn Coffee

Many Indian tribes often used corn for coffee. It is not unlike coffee in taste and is good if it is not too strong.

Take whole ears of husked corn, dry them thoroughly and roast them on hot coals. Then pound the kernels and boil them. Maple sugar was used to sweeten this rather strong drink.

Sunflower Coffee

The Seneca Indians used to prefer sunflower seeds for coffee. They roasted the seeds, pounded them, then separated the seeds from the shells and poured water over the seeds to get a coffee-like extract.

Again maple sugar was used to sweeten this bitter drink.

Chicory Coffee

The root of this common plant is used even today as an adjunct to coffee to give it a deeper color and a more lasting flavor and aroma. Chicory is a native of Europe and probably was imported as an impurity with seeds the settlers brought with them.

Chicory roots from spring-planted seeds are dried and then roasted and ground. This makes a good hot drink and was frequently used by the settlers. The addition of maple sugar vastly improves the flavor of this kind of coffee.

Sassafras Tea

The roots from the sassafras tree that grows in the southern part of the United States or from the sassafras bush in the northeastern part of the United States and Canada were used by the Iroquois Indians to make tea. As a matter of fact, the roots were of great importance for medicine and a whole expedition was sent out from England in 1602 to the New World to gather this plant.

The medicine produced by infusing the bark in water supposedly cured the ague. A tea made of the young shoots and roots was often used by early settlers to cure colds.

To prepare sassafras tea, cut the roots into small pieces and boil them with maple sugar in water to get a very pleasant drink.

New Jersey Tea

The leaves from *Ceanothus americanus*, popularly called the New Jersey tea bush, are common from Canada to the Gulf states. This bush is perhaps the best known beverage bush on the continent. It was commonly used as a substitute for tea during the American Revolutionary War.

Collect the leaves and dry them in the shade. This tea has a bitter taste not unlike ordinary tea. Steep the leaves as you would ordinary tea leaves.

Labrador Tea

A kind of low growing evergreen with the Latin name of *Ledum groenlandicum*, it is widely distributed in the northern latitudes of America. The leaves from this bush were also used as a tea substitute during the Revolution. *Ledium Patustre* also known as march tea or wild rosemary was used as a tea substitute by Sir John Franklin during his Arctic expedition of 1819-1822.

The leaves possess narcotic properties. The narrow leathery leaves have their margins rolled back with rusty wool on the undersides. Pluck the leaves, dry them and steep as you would ordinary tea.

Strawberry Leaf Tea

Tea made from dried strawberry leaves is a good remedy for colds. Pluck the young strawberry plant's leaves and dry them close to the fire. When dry use as you would ordinary tea but remember to steep a little longer.

Wintergreen Tea

The name wintergreen is applied to many plants which retain their foliage during the winter. The name wintergreen usually refers to the aromatic plant *Gaultheria procumbens* which is a low growing shrub barely six inches tall with creeping stems and ovate, glossy leathery leaves.

To use as tea, pluck the whole plant, stem, leaf and berry, pour boiling water over it and steep for about 15 minutes. This makes an excellent aromatic tea.

Indian Chocolate

The Indians and the early settlers used to make a chocolate tasting drink from the reddish brown root stalks of the white or purple avens *(Geum rivale)*, a marsh plant with lyre-shaped leaves and nodding purple flowers. The root stocks have astringent and tonic properties with a clove-like aroma. The word chocolate is misleading as it has been named more for the color than for taste.

Boil the root stocks in milk with maple sugar and you can pretend you are drinking chocolate.

Cherry or Black Birch Tea

Tea steeped from the bark of the cherry or black birch tree tastes identical to that of wintergreen tea. To make the tea, steep the bark or young twigs in hot water for about 15 minutes and you will have a tasty drink.

Sumac Lemonade

The fruit of the staghorn sumac (*Rhushirta*) was frequently used by Indians and pioneers to make a cool, sour drink. The name staghorn comes from the likeness of the down-covered branches to deer's antlers.

The fruit clusters are plucked and boiled in water, strained and sugar is added to give the juice an agreeable lemonade-like flavor.

Bear Berry or Service Berry Cider

Pick the berries of this plant, scald them until they are soft and crush them. To each quart of pulp add an equal amount of water. Strain through a cloth. When the juice is cool, a very spicy, acid but pleasant cider is ready.

Chapter 12

SUGAR AND SYRUPS

Nature has provided us with a great variety of sugars and syrups. In the days when sugar was an expensive item, our early settlers often tried to make their sugar go further by using substitutes from local sources.

MAPLE SYRUP

Maple sugar and syrup probably were one of the greatest gifts from the Indians to the pioneers.

The sugar maple (*Acer saccharum*) was widely used for collecting maple sap, but other maples also render a good sap, such as the silver maple, ash-leaved maple and red maple.

Although the exact details of the origin of the maple industry are not known, it is recorded that the early explorers found Indians drawing sap from the maple tree by cutting a V-shaped notch in the tree and inserting at the point of the V an elder spout. The sap was collected in birch bark containers and boiled down to sugar or syrup.

This method was crude and rendered a dark colored sugar. Now we know that if the sap is collected as often as possible and boiled down without delay, we get a better product which has not started to sour because of the sun's rays.

When you first start to collect maple sap don't get discouraged. You will need thirty to forty gallons of sap to produce one gallon of syrup.

In the early days, huge iron pots were placed on top of a blazing fire. In this way the water was removed from the sap. The temperature of the boiling sap should be 218 degrees F. Regional sap contains about ninety-six per cent water and must be boiled down a great deal to attain the density required for syrup. To get soft maple sugar, the sap is boiled to a higher temperature than for syrup. It is then cooled to about 100°F., stirred until it is a dull yellow color, and poured into moulds. We have evidence that the Ojibway Indians made birch bark cones to hold soft maple sugar.

Hard maple sugar is boiled to a slightly higher temperature than soft maple sugar and is cooled rapidly. When it starts to crystallize, the syrup is stirred until it becomes cloudy, yellowish and very thick. The sugar is then poured into moulds.

Maple syrup has many uses; as a sweetener on breads, pancakes, french toast, breakfast cereals and fruits.

It can also be used as a glaze on meats especially on ham, or on vegetables and fruits such as apples, pears and peaches.

I have often enjoyed maple syrup as a cold or hot sauce. If you intend to use it hot, let it boil for no more than 3 minutes and then pour it over cottage cheese, pudding, ice cream, custard or any other puddings.

Maple sugar is usually used as a sweetener in desserts, milk drinks, coffee. It can also be used on top of puddings, pancakes or hot buttered toast.

Maple sugar can also be used for all kinds of baking, simply substituting it for the sugar in the recipe.

When you need containers for storing syrup, use small glass jars or containers, as the syrup loses its fragrant flavor rapidly after the container has been opened. If you have been lucky enough to obtain a whole gallon of maple syrup, as soon as you get home, place the syrup in a large kettle and bring to a rolling boil for several minutes, then bottle in sterilized pint sealers or other jars of convenient size.

SUGAR PINE

The Indians on the west coast often used the sugar pine (*Pinus lambertiana*) to extract sugar. If the tree is injured, the sap bleeds and forms large lumps of a white sugary substance. If boiled down in water and skimmed of all impurities, it gives you a fairly good sugar substitute. But as this sugar has a laxative effect, it should be used in moderation.

BULRUSH SUGAR

In places where there were no maple sugar trees the Indians often used the bulrush root boiled down in water to make a weak sugar solution. But as it took a great deal of labor and the result wasn't entirely satisfactory, they preferred to trade with other tribes for maple sugar.

SCREW BEAN SUGAR

This spiny shrub or small tree of the family *Prosopis pupescens*, was used by Indians both for food and fodder. It was also used to make a weak sugar solution.

The pods were boiled down to make molasses and in this form made a satisfactory sweetener.

Chapter 13

WILDWOOD SEASONING

If you are on the trail or in camp for a prolonged period, you will find that you will run out of cooking spices.

Food without seasoning usually tastes very flat and does not enhance the appetite. The old saying, "Fresh air and hard labor is the best spice for your food," is not entirely true.

If you do run out of spices, nature provides a great variety of substitutes. But you must be able to recognize them and know how to prepare them.

The Indians very often used maple syrup and sugar to season their food. But in rare instances where deposits of natural salt were found, they were aware of its potential for seasoning.

If you find that you need extra seasonings in your camp kitchen here are a few plants which can be used to great advantage.

Coltsfoot Salt

Coltsfoot (*Tussilago farfara*) is often found along streams and in swamps. The plant is characterized by flowers which bloom before the leaves appear.

The flowers are yellow, the leaves are all basal, large and round with a heart-shaped base and lobed, toothed margins. The undersides of the leaves are covered with a dense felt-like substance.

To make salt, the Indians rolled the green leaves into small balls and placed them in the sun to dry. This took from 4 to 5 days. Then they put the dried balls on a flat stone and burned them to ashes. The ashes are very saline and make an excellent substitute for salt.

In fact, when you get used to this way of salting your food, it's hard to go back to ordinary salt.

Spice Bush — Allspice

The spice bush is an aromatic shrub (*Linders Benzoin*) which sometimes grows as tall as ten feet. The bush grows in damp woods and along stream banks. It is found in the eastern and central United States and Canada. The leaves are oval and turn a brilliant gold in the autumn.

Flowers are yellow, small, clustered and early-blooming. The twigs, leaves and fruit are all fragrant. When used as a spice, the bright red berries are thoroughly dried in the sun and then pounded to a powder which is used instead of allspice. The bush is also called the Benjamin bush, wild allspice and fever bush.

Wild Mint

Mint is a familiar flavor to all of us. It was used by the Indians long before the white man arrived on this continent.

The plant is characterized by square stems, opposite simple leaves and small, purple, white or pink, two-lipped auxiliary flowers in whorls which often form terminal spikes.

All mint varieties are noted for the fragrance of their foliage.

The most common species in North America are Canada mint (*Mentha arvensis*), spearmint (*Mentha spicata*) and peppermint (*Mentha piperita*).

All three varieties grow wild in the bush. I can't count the number of times this plant has spiced my wildwood menus. Never overlook this plant for enhancing any food. Indians also used the mint for vinegar.

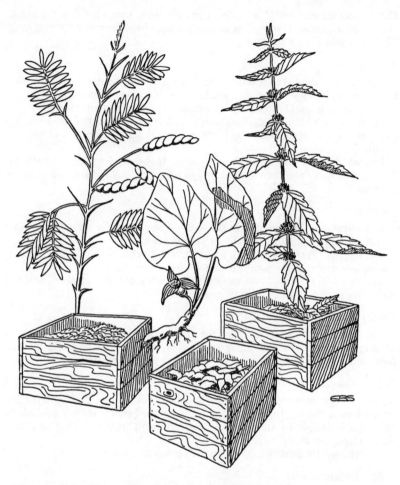

The young leaves can be eaten raw with salt or in salads. Mint can be cooked or added to any dish you prepare in the bush; for instance, boiled snake in mint sauce.

Wild Ginger

Wild ginger (*Asarum canadense*) or as it is sometimes called, Canada snake-root, is a small genus of herbs of the family *Aristolochiaceae* and is widely distributed in the northern hemisphere.

This plant prefers rich shady woods and has odd chocolate or purplish bell-shaped three-lobed perianths containing twelve horned stamens. The flowers, borne close to the ground are often hidden by the heart-shaped leaves.

The flowers are plucked and boiled in water. The solution is then boiled down to the right consistency until it has a strong smell of ginger. The root can also be scraped and boiled in water. The solution is then placed in the sun to evaporate. The powder is used as ordinary ginger but it is not quite as strong, so the amount should be doubled.

Wintergreen

This name is applied to several evergreen plants but the name usually refers to *Gaultheria procumbens* or, in some localities it is referred to as checkerberry.

The plant is a low shrub barely six inches tall, found in rocky woods. It has creeping stems, half hidden, from which arise erect reddish branches bearing ovate glossy leathery leaves. The fruits are bright scarlet, mealy and spicy in flavor.

The whole plant may be used for spicing. However, I prefer to crush the berries, boil them and then strain through a cheesecloth and use the fluid for cooking.

Sweet Bay

The sweet bay of America is the small tree, *Magnolia virginiana*, more frequently called swamp magnolia or swamp laurel.

The red bay (*Persea borbonia*), a small tree with reddish bark and evergreen leaves, is a native of the southwestern United States.

The leaves are plucked and sun-dried until they crumble easily. The dried leaves are used to flavor stuffings or soups.

Cherry Birch

The bark from this tree contains the same aromatic oil which is present in wintergreen. The buds and young twigs were used by Indians to flavor their food and a very fine tasting tea can be brewed from the twigs.

Indian Vinegar

Wild vinegar was made by several Indian tribes. It was derived from the fruit juices or the sap from the sugar maple or the birch tree. It is possible to make good vinegar by allowing the juice or sap to ferment in the sun, then strain through a cloth.

The vinegar fly usually looks after the fermentation for you.

Wild Mustard

The seeds from the black mustard plant (*Brassica nigra*) were often used by Indians or pioneers to sprinkle on their food for additional flavor.

These plants are annuals, often reaching four to six feet in height. All the leaves have stalks. The lower leaves are large and deeply lobed, but the upper leaves are small and toothed. Flowers are yellow and in long racemes; the seed pods are four-angled and stand erect to the stem.

The seeds are dried and pounded to a fine powder, then used as ordinary mustard.

Chapter 14

WILDERNESS COOKERY

The first part of this book has dealt with wilderness cooking; now we will talk about wilderness cookery.

The fine art of wilderness cookery was practiced by pioneer women in their crude kitchens, sometimes without even a stove. Nevertheless many excellent dishes were created.

Many of the dishes in this part of the book are hundreds of years old. Many date back several hundred years, having originated in Europe and brought to the New World by the early settlers. Often the supplies in the New World were not the same, so improvisations had to be made with native vegetables and meat.

You will find that for the most part we have selected recipes with ingredients from the wilderness or from the settlers' vegetable gardens.

A tremendous amount of credit has to go the early gourmet cooks who had the foresight and the courage to try out so many different and, to them, strange ingredients in their daily cooking, although much was learned from the Indians.

It is too bad that many of the old ways of preparing food have been forgotten, but in this book we have tried to bring back a little of the spirit of bygone days.

Of course it often takes many hours of loving care to produce one dish, but you will derive a great deal of satisfaction from making one of these old-fashioned dishes to surprise your family or guests.

To make this part of the book easy to follow and easy to find any specific recipe, it has been divided into four chapters; meat, birds, fish and desserts.

BEAR

Bear hunting is a widely practiced sport but unfortunately much bear meat is wasted because so few people appreciate the taste of bear meat.

The meat from brown, grizzly, and polar bear is rich, tender and delicious. The meat is at its prime early in the fall just before the bear goes into hibernation.

Late in the fall, a bear gorges himself on berries, various wild roots and fish to store up a reserve for the long winter sleep. Young animals, three years or less, are the tastiest.

Many people do not like the gamy taste of bear meat. If you want to remove this taste, marinating or smoking the meat is the answer. Also, if you don't like the taste of the fat, trim it off.

Most of the gamy taste is in the fat, and as bear meat is not marbled with fat, it is a simple matter to remove it.

Bear meat should always be well cooked until well-done to kill any trichinae which may be present. As with pork, it is risky to eat bear meat pink or rare.

All the Indians and trappers that I have known like to use bear fat for cooking or pastry making, but the fat must be rendered as soon as possible as it goes rancid quickly.

Rendering bear fat is quite easy — just cut the suet and surface fat into cubes. Place in a heavy cast iron pot, then heat the pot slowly and strain the fat. Bring the remainder of the liquid fat to a boil and simmer for 15 minutes, skimming off the top frequently.

Pour the sterilized fat into a sterilized glass container òr an earthenware crock. Seal absolutely airtight and store in a cool spot.

PEA SOUP WITH BEAR MEAT

While visiting old friends, trapper and guide Edward Big Belly and his wife, I was served a pea soup I will long remember. Here is their recipe.

2 cups dried yellow·peas	1 pound smoked bear ham
5 cups cold water	1 teaspoon pepper
2 wild onions, finely chopped	3 teaspoons salt
2 wild onions, whole	2 sweet bay leaves

Wash peas in cold running water and place them in a two to three-quart saucepan. Add five cups of water and bring to a boil over high heat. Boil briskly for 5 minutes, take the peas off the heat, cover, and let stand for at least one hour.

Skim off any pea husks which may have risen to the surface and add the chopped onions, whole onions, smoked bear ham, pepper, salt and bay leaves. Bring to a boil, then lower the heat and simmer with the pot partially covered for 1½ hours, until the peas are tender but have not fallen apart. Remove the whole onions and smoked bear ham from the soup. Cut the smoked bear ham into one-quarter inch-thick slices, and place in serving bowls. Cover with pea soup and serve as hot as possible. Instead of whole peas, the domestic split yellow peas can be used, but these do not need soaking and the cooking time can be shortened.

BEAR MEAT FILLED ARROWHEAD TUBERS

I remember this dish from the time when I was a small boy accompanying my father on an inspection trip to a lonely charcoal kiln.

1 pint arrowhead tubers, mashed	¾ cup flour
1 egg	¼ teaspoon baking powder
2 tablespoons milk	1 teaspoon sugar
1 teaspoon salt	2 cups lean, smoked bear meat

In a mixing bowl, mix the arrowhead tubers, egg, milk and salt. Sift the flour, baking powder and sugar over the batter and mix well. Cube the bear meat into small cubes and place in the frying pan. Fry until well browned. Remove from heat and cool. Take a heaping tablespoon of the batter into well floured hands and make a patty about three inches in diameter. Place a rounded tablespoon of the cubed bear meat in the center of the patty and close it by folding outer edges over the filling in the center.

Fill a two to three quart saucepan three-quarters full with cold water, add two teaspoons of salt and bring to a boil.

Drop the patties into the salted water three or four at a time and cook for 20 minutes.

If you have some bear meat left in the frying pan, add two tablespoons of flour and a cup of milk to it, and make a sauce which can be poured over the patties when served.

Arrowhead tubers can be replaced by cold mashed potatoes and lean bacon substituted for the bear meat.

SMOKED BEAR HAM AND WILD RICE BALLS

2 pounds smoked bear ham, ground	1 egg
2 cups wild rice	2 tablespoons flour
1 teaspoon salt	1 teaspoon pepper

Place the wild rice in a two quart saucepan, adding enough water to cover the rice. Boil uncovered for 30 minutes and remove from heat. In a small bowl mix the egg, flour and a little water. Add the egg mixture to the boiled rice, mix well and add the ground smoked bear meat.

Make into small balls and place in a greased nine by nine inch casserole and bake for about 1½ hours at 325 degrees F. Serve with applesauce.

SMOKED BEAR HAM WITH HONEY AND MAPLE SYRUP GLAZE

The bear hunt had been successful the year I visited my old trapper friend, Indian Joe. The smokehouse went full blast for over a week. One morning he brought in a freshly smoked bear ham, to be prepared for supper. This is how he cooked it.

1 bear ham, smoked (8 to 10 pounds)	½ cup maple syrup
1 teaspoon spice bush powder	¼ cup dried breadcrumbs
½ cup wild honey	¼ cup hazelnuts, finely chopped

Remove rind from the ham, being careful not to remove any of the fat. Using a sharp knife score almost through the fat. Sprinkle the spice bush powder all over the ham.

In a bowl, thoroughly mix the wild honey, maple syrup and bread crumbs. Smear the glaze all over the ham and place the ham on a baking dish in a 375 degree F. oven for 30 minutes, basting occasionally.

Remove the ham from the oven, ice with a heavy coat of glaze sprinkled with chopped hazelnuts, then place the ham back in the oven at 425 degrees F. for about 5 minutes to set the glaze.

Serve either hot with arrowhead tubers or potatoes, or serve cold cut into one-quarter inch slices.

MARINATED BEAR STEAKS

Meat from a bear killed just before hibernation is usually rich, tender and delicious. But, if the gamy taste is objectionable, all fat should be trimmed off as the fat holds most of this taste. Bear meat is not marbled with fat like top grade beef, so trimming the fat is quite easy.

Marinating the meat lessens the gamy taste, and at the same time makes the meat tender and juicy.

4 bear steaks, 1½ inches thick
2 wild onions, sliced
1 cup Indian vinegar
1 cup water

½ cup maple syrup
2 tablespoons spice bush powder
1 tablespoon salt
1 tablespoon bear fat, rendered
Salt and pepper

In a large glass or pottery bowl mix the onions, Indian vinegar, water, maple syrup, spice bush powder and salt. Let stand for a couple of hours, then put in the bear steaks. Place in a cool place for at least 24 hours, turning the steaks from time to time.

Remove the steaks from the marinade, let them drain and pat dry. Heat a heavy frying pan and rub the pan with the rendered bear fat. Place the steaks in the pan and sear on both sides.

Lower the heat and finish cooking, adding more fat to prevent sticking. Remove the steaks from the frying pan. Add a little flour and water to thicken the gravy. Pour gravy over the individual steaks on the serving dish.

Serve with potatoes.

BEAVER

The industrious beaver is the largest rodent on the North American continent. He is usually trapped for the sake of the pelt, but let me give you several superb dishes made with beaver meat.

The meat is dark red, fine-grained, tender and moist and the taste of beaver meat is not unlike the taste of roast pork.

Beaver tail soup is rated high on the gourmet's list of delightful dishes. The meat in the tail is white and tender.

When skinning the beaver carcass, care should be taken that the tiny musk glands from under the skin on the inside of the legs, and the castor gland under the belly near the tail are removed carefully. Make sure that the skinning knife is properly cleaned after this operation, as a dirty knife could spoil the rest of the meat.

The Assiniboine Indians had an easy way of removing the scaly skin on the tail. They broiled the tails over the camp fire and the scaly skin came off in blistered sheets to reveal the white, solid meat.

The taste of beaver tail meat is considered to have the combined flavor of salt pork and finnan haddie. To me it has a delightful flavor all its own.

BEAVER TAIL SOUP

This recipe was the specialty of a long time friend and hunting companion, Ian Paterson who was considered to be an expert in beaver tail soup.

Bones from a beaver	4 sweet bay leaves
1 beaver tail	1 tablespoon wild mustard
4 wild onions	1 tablespoon spice bush powder
4 quarts water	1 tablespoon salt

Separate the bones from the meat, break the bones into six inch pieces. Skin the tail as described above, and cut the meat into six inch lengths. Put the bones and pieces of the tail in a large kettle, add the water and salt. Bring to a boil, lower the heat and simmer for 30 minutes. With a large spoon, keep the surface clean from scum and then add the sliced onions, bay leaves, wild mustard and spice bush powder. Continue to simmer for another 30 minutes.

Remove the beaver tail pieces. Let drain on a plate and set aside to be added to the soup at a later time. Strain the soup through a fine sieve into another large pot and boil down to about a quarter of its original volume. Clarify with the white from one egg.

Cut the meat from the tail into cubes about one-half inch square, add to the soup and serve hot. If you wish, garnish with fresh finely-cut mint sprinkled over the individual servings.

SAUTÉED BEAVER TAILS

This recipe was given to me by an old trapper, whose name has been long forgotten.

1 beaver tail, skinned	2 tablespoons spice bush powder
2 cups Indian vinegar	1 cup wheat flour
2 cups water	1 tablespoon wild mustard
1 tablespoon salt	1 teaspoon spice bush powder
4 wild onions, sliced	4 wild onions, finely chopped
4 sweet bay leaves	4 wild apples, cubed

Skin the tail by searing it over an open fire and remove the blistered scaled skin. Cut into two inch pieces and place in a large soup kettle. Add the vinegar, water, salt, onion, bay leaves and spice bush powder. Bring to a boil, lower heat and let simmer for about 30 minutes. Remove from the heat and strain through a fine sieve, discarding the juice. Cover the meat with fresh water and let come to a boil, then simmer for 15 minutes. Remove from heat, drain off all the juices and pat dry on a paper towel or freshly cut evergreen boughs.

Place a large frying pan or skillet on the stove, then add the finely chopped onions and some fat. Fry until the onions are golden brown. Remove pan from heat.

Mix flour, mustard, spice bush powder and salt. Roll the two-inch pieces of beaver tail in the flour mixture and place in the hot frying pan. Sear both sides until brown. Add the fried onions and apples and cook for about 15 minutes covered. Serve hot with creamed onions.

CREAMED WILD ONIONS

20 small wild onions	2 cups milk
4 tablespoons flour	1 teaspoon salt
4 tablespoons butter	½ teaspoon pepper

Melt the butter in a small saucepan. Add the flour, stirring constantly. When the butter and flour form small balls in the pan, add the milk slowly. Then add the salt and pepper and simmer for 15 minutes. Meanwhile, peel and wash the wild onions. In another saucepan, cover them with water and bring to a boil. Boil for about 15 minutes or until the onions are tender. Remove from heat and drain. Add the onions to the white sauce and simmer for a few minutes.

STUFFED MARINATED BEAVER HAM

While visiting a beaver trapper in Quebec, his wife served this truly delicious dish.

Use a long narrow skinning knife to cut all around the bone in the ham. Remove the bone, leaving a round hole. As my visit was in late winter while the sap was running, the ham was placed in an earthenware crock and covered with maple sap. It was then kept in a cool place for 48 hours. The ham was then removed from the marinade and patted dry.

STUFFING

3 cups cooked wild rice	1 tablespoon bulrush shoots,
2 tablespoons wild onion,	finely chopped
finely chopped	1 tablespoon minced bacon
½ cup beef bouillon	1 teaspoon salt

Combine the cooked rice, wild onion, bouillon and bulrush shoots. Mix well and set aside. In a frying pan, brown the bacon slightly then add the rice mixture and salt. Sauté lightly until the mixture appears fluffy.

2 beaver hams	½ cup Indian vinegar
½ cup dry mustard	1 teaspoon salt
½ cup brown sugar	½ teaspoon pepper

Trim the beaver hams of all fat and rub the outside and the hole in the hams with salt and pepper. In a small bowl mix the mustard, sugar and vinegar to a smooth paste.

Fill the hole in the hams with the stuffing, then smear the mustard mixture on the outside of the hams. Place in a roasting pan and bake at a temperature of 375 degrees F. for 2 hours or until fluid is clear when the meat is pierced with the tip of a sharp knife. Remove from the oven and let stand for 5 minutes before cutting the ham into one-half inch thick slices.

ROASTED BEAVER

Roast beaver was one of Homer Blais' favorite dishes when he was on his trapline during the winter. Many a time I have enjoyed beaver prepared in this way in his shanty in the Canadian wilderness.

1 beaver, cleaned and washed	2 large wild onions, sliced
1 cup Indian vinegar	6 strips salt pork
1 tablespoon coarse salt	½ teaspoon salt
2 tablespoons baking soda	½ teaspoon pepper

Place the beaver in a large enameled soup kettle, add the vinegar and coarse salt, cover with cold water and let stand overnight. The next morning, remove the beaver from the pot and discard the marinade. Place the beaver in the cleaned pot, add water to cover, and baking soda. Bring to a boil and simmer for 20 minutes. Remove from heat and cool in the juice. When cool, remove the beaver from the pot and place belly down in a large roasting pan with a lid.

Place slices of onion and salt pork on the back of the beaver. Sprinkle salt and pepper over the meat. Cover the roasting pan and place in a preheated oven at 375 degrees F. for about 3 hours, or until the meat is tender. Serve with tart apple jelly and vegetables.

BEAVER SOUP STOCK

When visiting Indian villages I found that Indians often use beaver to make soup stock which enhances the stock with a wild gamy taste.

3 pounds beaver bones and meat	1 cup wild onions
½ cup bacon fat	1 tablespoon salt
3 quarts cold water	¼ cup shredded mint
½ cup cattail shoots	2 tablespoons spice bush powder
1 cup arrowhead tubers	2 sweet bay leaves

Wipe the meat clean and remove all fat and meat from the bones. Melt the bacon fat in a heavy frying pan, then brown the meat on all sides. Place bones and the browned meat in a large soup kettle and cover with cold water. Add the peeled arrowhead tubers, cattail shoots, mint, spice bush powder and bay leaves. Cover the kettle and bring to a boil. Reduce heat and simmer for 4 to 5 hours. Strain through a fine sieve and cool. When the liquid has cooled, remove the fat from the surface and strain again. Store in a cool place.

DANDELION SOUP

Here is a soup made out of beaver stock and served on early spring mornings by Indian Joe's wife.

4 tablespoons rendered bear fat	4 cups beaver stock
2 wild onions, finely chopped	½ teaspoon salt
1 cup arrowhead tubers, finely chopped	½ teaspoon pepper
2 cups young dandelion leaves	

Melt the bear fat in a heavy saucepan on top of the stove. When the bear fat is sizzling hot, add the finely chopped onions and simmer until onions are translucent but not brown. Add the arrowhead tubers and dandelion leaves and heat for 5 minutes. Add the soup stock, salt and pepper. Bring to a boil. Reduce heat and simmer for 15 minutes.

Serve hot with freshly baked bannock.

BUFFALO

EBS

This Indian and pioneer source of food had almost disappeared by the early 1920's, but before the turn of the century great herds of buffalo roamed the western plains.

Even after domestic cattle were introduced, Indians still depended heavily on the buffalo hunt for their food.

Thanks to conservation measures which proved effective we late comers to this continent still can get buffalo meat if we are lucky. Every year some buffalo are killed in one of the buffalo sanctuaries and the meat is commercially sold all over this continent. If you find that your butcher's selling buffalo, don't ignore this opportunity, but buy it and try it.

The meat from young buffalo is tender, fine-grained and similar in taste to top grade beef, but it is darker in color. The meat from older animals usually lacks the fat that younger animals have, and it may be necessary to lard the meat.

Buffalo meat can be prepared as you would beef, but you have to remember to lengthen the cooking time by about one-third. To lard the meat, use a larding needle and use fresh suet, cut in long thin strips. This operation is easier if the suet is chilled.

BRAISED BUFFALO STEAK

During a visit to the Northwest Territories, I was a house guest at a Hudson Bay station. The manager's wife had been lucky enough to secure six round steaks of buffalo which she prepared in the following manner.

6 buffalo steaks, 1 inch thick	1 teaspoon salt
Salt, pepper, flour for coating	½ teaspoon pepper
the steaks.	½ tablespoon brown sugar
3 tablespoons bacon fat	2 bay leaves
2 cups onions, sliced	1½ tablespoons mint, finely
1 tablespoon flour	chopped
1½ tablespoons vinegar	2 cups stale beer

Melt bacon fat in a heavy iron frying pan. When the fat is sizzling hot, sear the dusted steaks on both sides. Remove from pan and set aside. Add the onions to the remaining fat in the pan and sauté until golden brown. Add flour, making sure that it has dissolved in the onion-fat mixture before adding the vinegar, salt, pepper, brown sugar, bay leaves, mint and beer. Simmer for 15 minutes. Place the steaks in a large casserole that can hold them comfortably without crowding. Pour the onion sauce over the steaks, and cover.

Place the casserole in the oven and cook at 350 degrees F. for 2½ hours. Serve with boiled, unpeeled potatoes and lingonberries.

ROAST BUFFALO WITH GOAT CHEESE SAUCE

This is my favorite recipe for buffalo meat.

4 pounds boneless haunch of	2 teaspoons salt
buffalo	1 teaspoon pepper
3 tablespoons bacon fat, softened	1½ cups beef stock

Preheat the oven to 375 degrees F. Tie the roast neatly at one-half inch intervals with kitchen string. With a pastry brush, spread the fat evenly over the roast. Heat a large iron frying pan on top of the stove over high heat until a drop of water bounces when dropped in the frying pan. Sear the roast on all sides until it is dark brown. Place the roast in a shallow open roasting pan with rack, and sprinkle generously with salt and pepper. Pour the beef stock in the pan and place it in the preheated oven uncovered for 1½ hours, basting frequently with a bulb baster. The center meat, when finished, should be slightly rare, or register about 150 degrees on a meat thermometer. Transfer the roast to a heated platter, cover loosely with foil and put it back in the turned-off oven until served.

GOAT CHEESE SAUCE

1 teaspoon butter	1 ounce Norwegian goat cheese
1 tablespoon flour	½ cup sour cream
2 teaspoons red currant jelly	

Skim and discard the fat from the pan juices. Measure the remaining liquid and either reduce to a cup by boiling, or add enough water to make one cup. In a small heavy saucepan, heat one tablespoon of butter and stir in the flour, stirring constantly with a wooden spoon. Cook this roux for 8 to 10 minutes over low heat until it is a nut-brown color. Be careful not to let it burn as this will give the sauce a bitter taste.

Add the cup of pan juices and with a wire whisk beat to a smooth roux. Add the currant jelly and the finely grated cheese. Beat until the jelly and the cheese are completely dissolved, then stir in the sour cream. Do not let the sauce boil.

Taste for seasoning. Remove the strings from the roast and carve into thin slices. Serve with boiled arrowhead tubers or potatoes, carrots and peas. Serve the sauce from a gravy boat, separately.

BUFFALO MEAT BALLS

If you get one of the tougher cuts of buffalo meat, it can be used for delightfully different meat balls. Here is the way I prepare them.

2 pounds buffalo meat	2 onions, finely chopped
½ pound suet	1 teaspoon salt
2 slices white bread	½ teaspoon pepper
2 eggs	2 tablespoons bacon fat
1 cup milk	

Run the buffalo meat and the suet through a meat mincer twice. Set aside. Put the bread, with the crust removed into a large bowl, add the milk and soak for 15 minutes.

Add the eggs, onion, salt, pepper and ground meat to the milk and bread. Knead the mixture until all the ingredients are well mixed.

Using a large frying pan, melt some of the bacon fat and heat well. Make small balls (the balls should not be more than one-half inch in diameter) with your hands and drop them into the the frying pan. Sear until lightly browned. The easy way to do this is not to crowd the pan, but to shake it constantly so the balls roll around. When all the mixture is used up, lower the heat, cover the frying pan and cook for about 20 minutes. Stir occasionally to prevent the meatballs from getting too brown. They are delicious as a snack or as part of a buffet dinner.

CARIBOU

Caribou is the name given to two or more species of reindeer inhabiting Canada. They are a very important source of food and clothing to the natives of the arctic and sub-arctic regions. As a general rule, two kinds of caribou are recognized — the barren-land caribou and the woodland caribou.

Their semi-annual migrations mean harvest for Eskimos and Northern Indians. A successful hunt means a comfortable winter for these people. But slaughter of the caribou has been so widespread, that even on the barren grounds these herds are now small and scattered. The obvious reason for this has been the introduction of guns to the Eskimos and Indians.

Every edible part of the animal, even the entrails and bone marrow, is eaten. From the bones and horns various implements are made, while the hide makes good clothing and bedding.

During the summer, caribou feed on lichens, grasses dwarf shrubs and flowering plants. Because of their diet and their leisurely roaming habits, the caribou's meat is tender and tasty. However, the meat is lean and usually needs to be larded before it is cooked.

This is how I lard all lean wild game.

I prefer to use salt pork. The pork is cut into long strips one-quarter inch wide and one-quarter inch thick and is put in the freezer to be thoroughly chilled before use. Then I thread the larding needle with a strip of pork and run the needle through the meat, letting the pork protrude about half an inch on both ends. Thread the strips about two inches apart all through the roast.

If you don't have a larding needle, you can get the same effect by piercing the meat with a long thin knife and pushing the pork through the meat. But as this is time consuming and the results are not always satisfactory, I recommend that you use a larding needle.

BRAISED STUFFED CARIBOU HEART

This is a delicacy I make from a freshly killed caribou. However, a heart is hard to come by if the killing has been done by an Eskimo, as he will cut out the still warm heart and devour it raw.

1 caribou heart	1 teaspoon salt
2 tablespoons salt	1 teaspoon spice bush powder
1½ cup bannock, dried	½ teaspoon pepper
½ cup onion, finely chopped	2 cups beef broth
½ cup cattail shoots, diced	1 cup cattail shoots, diced
½ cup cooked bacon, crumbled	2 wild onions, whole
1 egg, slightly beaten	6 stalks wild leeks, bulb
2 tablespoons evaporated milk	and greens

Wash heart thoroughly, wipe with a damp cloth and cut away fat and small thread-like cords. Sprinkle inside and out with salt. Place the heart in a large glass jar and sprinkle with the rest of the salt. Add enough water to cover the heart and let stand overnight in a cool place.

The next morning drain the heart thoroughly and wash in cold water. Combine the crumbled bannock, onion, cattail shoots, bacon, egg, salt, spice bush powder, pepper and the evaporated milk to make a loose stuffing.

Fill opening with the stuffing and lace together loosely with skewers and twine. Place the heart in a Dutch oven and add two cups of beef broth. Cover and simmer for 3 hours or until almost tender. Add the diced cattail shoots, peeled onions and leeks. Cover again and continue simmering until tender.

Remove the heart and keep warm. Strain the juices through a fine sieve and return the strained juice to the Dutch oven.

Mix two tablespoons flour with two tablespoons of water to each cup of broth and add the flour-water mixture to the juice with constant stirring. Serve with boiled rice, or even better, wild rice if you have any.

CARIBOU POT ROAST

In northern Quebec one quite often finds handwritten cookbooks which have been in a family for hundreds of years. The following recipe originated in France in 1705 and was brought to the New World in 1840. You can see the use of local game and meat.

5 pounds boneless round roast of caribou	4 cloves
2 teaspoons salt	1 cup red wine
½ teaspoon black pepper	4 tablespoons wine vinegar
¼ teaspoon nutmeg	2 tablespoons bacon fat
1 wild onion, sliced	2 tablespoons brandy
1 carrot, sliced	1 garlic clove, crushed
3 mint leaves	2 bay leaves
2 bay leaves, crushed	Carrots, wild onions, potatoes
1 teaspoon spice bush powder	Chantrelle mushrooms
	2 tablespoons flour

Rub the roast with the salt, pepper and nutmeg. Place the roast in a large earthenware crock, then add one sliced onion, one sliced carrot, three crushed mint leaves, two crushed bay leaves, spice bush powder, a clove, red wine and wine vinegar. Add enough water to barely cover the roast. Cover the crock and keep it in a cool place overnight, turning the roast two or three times.

Drain meat, strain and save the marinade. Melt the bacon fat in a Dutch oven and brown the roast on all sides over high heat on top of the stove. Add half of the strained marinade, brandy, garlic and bay leaves. Cover the Dutch oven tightly and simmer on top of the stove for 3 hours or until the meat is tender. During this time turn the roast over at least twice. Add ten small well-cleaned carrots, six small wild onions, ten small peeled potatoes and one-half pound cleaned and halved chantrelle mushrooms. Cover and continue to simmer for another 45 minutes. Remove the roast and put on a heated platter. Arrange the carrots, onions and potatoes around the roast and put back in the oven to keep warm.

Skim the fat from the surface of the pan juices. Mix two tablespoons flour with the marinade, then add this mixture to the pan juices. Cook and stir until thickened.

If the meat comes from an older animal it is necessary to lard the roast after marinating it.

CARIBOU HASH WITH RAW EGGS

This recipe comes from the same cookbook and makes an interesting breakfast dish. Fried eggs may be substituted for raw eggs.

4 cups potatoes, peeled and diced into ¼-inch pieces	2 tablespoons butter
2 cups caribou roast, diced into ¼-inch pieces	2 tablespoons bacon fat
1 cup salt pork, diced into ¼-inch pieces	3 small onions, finely chopped
	1 tablespoon mint, finely chopped
	1 teaspoon salt
	½ teaspoon pepper

Unlike most hashes, the potatoes, caribou meat, salt pork and onions are cooked separately to retain their individual character. Peel and cut the potatoes in cubes and place them in cool water to prevent them from discoloring. When ready to use, drain them in a colander and pat dry.

Melt the butter and bacon fat in a heavy frying pan over high heat. When the foam subsides, add the potatoes. Lower the heat to moderate, and fry the potatoes for about 20 minutes turning them in the pan with a spoon until they are brown and crisp. Remove them from the pan and set aside to drain on paper towels. Place the onions in the frying pan and fry until golden brown and transparent. Add the diced meat and salt pork, shaking the pan often so that the meat cubes brown lightly on all sides. Stir in the fried potatoes and heat until the potatoes are heated through.

Sprinkle the finely chopped mint, salt and pepper over the dish and stir until well mixed.

Arrange the hash in individual servings on heated plates. Make a depression in the hash and put the raw yolk there, or, if you wish, a fried egg.

STANDING RIB ROAST OF CARIBOU

When I visit Ole and his family, one dinner menu always includes a standing rib roast served with arrowhead tubers and creamed plantain leaves.

1 5-pound rib roast of caribou	**3 wild onions**
2 tablespoons bacon fat	**1 cup cattail shoots**
½ teaspoon salt	**1½ cups wild leeks, diced**
½ teaspoon pepper	**¼ cup dandelion roots, diced**
2 tablespoons flour	**1½ cups beef bouillon**

Wipe roast well with a damp cloth and trim off all excess fat. Rub all surfaces with the bacon fat, then sprinkle with salt, pepper and flour.

Place in a roaster adding the wild onions, cattail shoots, wild leeks, dandelion roots and bouillon. Cover well and cook in a preheated oven at 450 degrees F. for 30 minutes. Reduce the heat to 350 degrees F. and cook for at least 2 hours or until the meat is tender.

Remove the roast to a heated platter and put it back in the oven to keep warm. Strain the cooking juices into a saucepan. Dissolve two tablespoons of flour in a little water and add to the cooking juices. Let simmer for 10 minutes, stirring constantly. Season to taste with salt and pepper.

CREAMED PLANTAIN LEAVES

1 pound plantain leaves	**1½ cups milk**
3 tablespoons butter	**1 teaspoon salt**
3 tablespoons flour	**½ teaspoon white pepper**

Thoroughly clean and wash the plantain leaves. Cut the stems off and remove the veins from the back. Place in a saucepan, cover with water and bring to a boil. Lower the heat and simmer for 5 minutes. Remove from heat and drain in a colander. Pat dry between paper towels and chop fairly fine. Place the butter in a small saucepan and melt under high heat. Add the flour, stirring until the butter is completely absorbed by the flour, then add the milk, salt and pepper to the butter-flour mixture using a wire whisk to make a smooth creamy sauce or roux. Simmer on low heat for 15 minutes, making sure that the roux does not stick to the bottom of the pan. Add the finely chopped plantain leaves to the roux and simmer until the leaves are thoroughly heated.

BOILED ARROWHEAD TUBERS

Put about 24 medium arrowhead tubers, washed and scraped into a saucepan with one teaspoon salt and bring to a boil. Lower the heat and simmer for 30 minutes. Drain and transfer to a serving bowl.

The creamed plantain leaves and arrowhead tubers go well with the caribou rib roast.

CARIBOU MEAT AND VEGETABLE SOUP

There is good stewing meat on a caribou, and a delicious soup can be made from it.

2 pounds caribou stew meat	6 arrowhead tubers, cubed
½ pound salt pork, in a slab	3 wild onions
2 quarts cold water	3 wild leeks, bulbs and greens
1 dandelion root	½ teaspoon spice bush powder
6 bulrush shoots	1 teaspoon salt

Cook the salt pork in a large iron pot or Dutch oven over high heat on top of the stove for 10 minutes. Remove the pork and set aside. Add the caribou meat and brown on all sides. Add the water and salt pork, cover and simmer for 2 hours, skimming occasionally. Remove from heat and store in a cool place overnight. The next day remove half of the congealed fat from the surface and add the diced dandelion roots, diced bulrush shoots, arrowhead tubers, sliced onions, wild leeks, spice bush powder and salt. Bring to a boil, then lower heat and simmer for 2 hours. Serve as hot as possible in individual bowls, with dark rye bread.

DALL SHEEP

The white mountain-sheep of Alaska was unknown to the world until 1884. Since then it has become one of the world's most sought-after game trophies. The Dall sheep with its golden horns and its snow-white coat is the only known wild white sheep in existence. It inhabits the rugged Mackenzie Mountains of the Northwest Territories.

This virtually untouched mountain range, grazed by the white Dall appears to be an excellent place for trophy hunting. Wild sheep are not covered with wool like a domestic sheep. Next to the skin is a coat of fine woolly hair, which is for warmth, but over this is a coat of long coarse hair which serves as a raincoat for the sheep.

Mountain sheep cannot survive in captivity because of their delicate feeding habits, consequently they are almost unknown to the general public.

The sheep weigh about 150 to 200 pounds when mature and because they feed on sweet grass and lichens, their meat is tender and delicious. Like all lamb or mutton, the meat should be served either very hot or very cold.

MOUNTAIN SHEEP CASSEROLE

My wife makes this wonderful casserole of Dall lamb chops, arrowhead tubers and wild onions with cream.

6 Dall sheep chops, 1-inch thick	3 tablespoons mint, finely chopped
1 tablespoon bacon grease	3 tablespoons flour
6 medium arrowhead tubers, sliced	2 tablespoons bacon grease
6 medium wild onions, sliced	4 cups heavy cream
	Salt and pepper

Brown the chops on both sides in the bacon fat.

Thoroughly wash, scrape and slice the arrowhead tubers. Clean the wild onions and slice thinly. Wash the mint leaves and chop finely. Grease a shallow fireproof casserole, large enough to take the chops in one layer and arrange a layer of arrowhead tubers on the bottom of the casserole. Dot with bacon grease, sprinkle with some of the flour and mint, and cover this layer with wild onion slices. Repeat in layers until all the arrowhead tubers and onions are used up, finishing with a layer of arrowhead tubers. Sprinkle flour, salt and pepper between the layers. Top with the browned chops and pour the cream over all.

Bake in a 325 degree F. oven for 1½ hours. Serve from the casserole steaming hot.

DALL LAMB IN DILL SAUCE

Here is one of my favorite recipes for lamb. After a successful Dall sheep hunt in the Mackenzie Mountains I used this very old Swedish recipe.

4 pounds breast or shoulder of lamb, cut in 2-inch cubes	Bouquet of 2 sweet bay leaves, 10 sprigs of dill and 5 mint leaves tied together with a string
5 cups water	
1 tablespoon salt	
4 whole peppercorns	

In a large iron pot, cover the lamb with cold water and bring to a boil, uncovered, over high heat. Lower heat and skim off and discard the scum as it rises to the surface. Add the salt, pepper and bouquet. Partially cover the pot and simmer for 2 hours, or until the meat is tender.

Transfer the lamb to a deep, heated platter and return to the oven at 200 degrees F. to keep warm.

Strain the cooking juices through a fine sieve or colander and set aside.

DILL SAUCE

2 tablespoons butter
2 tablespoons flour
2½ cups lamb stock or
  cooking juice from roast
4 tablespoons fresh dill, chopped
1 tablespoon wine vinegar

2 teaspoons sugar
½ teaspoon salt
½ teaspoon lemon juice
1 egg yolk, lightly beaten
Dill crowns
Lemon slices

Boil down the strained cooking juices until reduced to two and a half cups.

Melt the butter in a small saucepan, add the two tablespoons of flour to the butter and stir well. Add the reduced lamb stock all at once to the butter-flour mixture. Stir rapidly with a wire whisk until the mixture is smooth and thick. Simmer sauce over low heat for 5 minutes, making sure that the sauce does not stick to the bottom of the pan.

Add the chopped dill, wine vinegar, salt, sugar and lemon juice. Heat thoroughly without boiling. Taste for seasoning; add salt and pepper if necessary. Remove the platter of lamb from the oven, pour the sauce over the lamb and garnish with wedges of lemon and sprigs of dill.

Serve with small buttered arrowhead tubers or with boiled rice.

DALL LAMB AND PLANTAIN LEAF CASSEROLE

On one of my first trips to the Northwest Territories this dish was served to me by a Norwegian trapper and hunter for the Hudson Bay Company. Ole told me that this recipe came from his great-grandmother and that he had adapted it to suit local conditions.

2 tablespoons bacon grease
4 pounds breast of lamb,
  trimmed of fat and cut
  into 2-inch cubes
½ cup flour
2 pounds plantain leaves

1 cup cattail shoots
2 cups wild onion, sliced
3 cups beef stock
2 tablespoons salt
2 tablespoons black pepper,
  crushed and tied in a
  cheesecloth bag

Preheat the oven to 350 degrees F. Melt the bacon fat in a large heavy skillet, and heat until the fat starts to smoke. Add the cubed meat and cook over medium high heat, turning the cubes with a spoon until they are browned on all sides.

Using a slotted spoon, transfer the meat from the skillet to a large mixing bowl, sprinkle with flour and stir slightly until all the meat is lightly coated and no trace of flour remains. Place the onions in the skillet and fry until they are golden brown. Remove from heat and set aside.

In a six-quart casserole with a cover, arrange a layer of meat in the bottom of the casserole and then a layer of plantain leaves. Sprinkle with half of the onions and diced cattail shoots. Salt each layer lightly. Repeat and end with a layer of plantain leaves. Place the skillet back on the fire with remains of the fat from the meat and pour into the skillet the beef stock, stirring constantly. Cook for 5 minutes, then pour the stock over the casserole. Place the bag of pepper on top, cover and cook in preheated oven for 2 hours or until the meat is tender. Serve hot with mint jelly.

ROAST STUFFED SHOULDER OF DALL LAMB

Ernie Roseen, guide and trapper, just as spry at seventy as the Dall sheep he hunts, not only taught me how to hunt the animal but also how to cook it afterwards. Here is how he prepares shoulder of Dall lamb.

5-6 pound shoulder of lamb	4 tablespoons onions, grated
1½ tablespoons salt	1 teaspoon spice bush powder
2/3 tablespoon pepper	2 cups bannock crumbs

Preheat the oven to 300 degrees F. Remove the bone from the shoulder by cutting all around it with a long, narrow filleting knife, cutting as close to the bone as possible.

Rub the inside and outside of the meat with all but one-half teaspoon salt and one-quarter teaspoon pepper. In a large mixing bowl, make the stuffing by mixing the bannock crumbs, onions, spice bush powder, salt and pepper. Add just enough water to moisten the mixture so it will hold together. If there are small pieces of meat stuck to the bone, remove them and add to the stuffing. Stuff the hole in the meat loosely with the stuffing and sew the edges of the hole together. Place the meat with fat side up on a rack in a deep roasting pan. Cook in the oven for 4 hours.

Serve steaming hot with potatoes and mint jelly.

MOTHER'S MINT JELLY

No mint jelly tastes as full-bodied as the one my mother makes.

3 cups fresh mint leaves	5 drops food coloring
3 cups water	3½ cups sugar
2 tablespoons lemon juice	½ bottle fruit pectin

Wash the leaves under running water and remove any that are wilted or bruised. Shred them into small pieces to release the oil.

In a large four to five-quart saucepan, bring the water to a quick boil. Add the mint leaves and cook for 2 minutes. Remove from heat, cover and let stand for at least 10 minutes.

Wash the saucepan. Measure one and three-quarter cups of strained mint juice into it, add two tablespoons strained lemon juice, the food coloring and sugar. Place the pan over low heat to dissolve the sugar. Increase the heat and bring the mixture to a boil, stirring constantly. Add the fruit pectin and bring to a full rolling boil for 1 minute, stirring constantly. Remove from heat. Remove all the scum from the surface with a metal spoon. Pour into sterilized jelly jars immediately.

Cover the surface quickly with one-eighth of an inch of melted paraffin. Cool and store in a cool place.

DEER

The deer family (*Cervidae*) is the best known of all our large game. The deer family is older than other families of ruminants, dating back to the Lower Miocene Period when deer were very small and without antlers.

Deer have been hunted since early times. Their meat, venison, is considered a delicacy.

The deer is valued not only for its meat, but for its skins which were used by the Indians for clothing and for covering their tepees and canoes. Deer hoofs and horns are prized for ornamental purposes.

According to Doctor Randolph L. Peterson, recent studies show that body growth takes precedence over antler development in young deer, so that larger, better fed deer grow larger antlers. The white-tailed deer is a New World species and is found throughout most of North America, south of a line from Anticosti Island in the Gulf of St. Lawrence to James Bay and westward; it extends through Central America to South America.

The mule deer is found in southern Manitoba and northern Minnesota. This deer is distinguished by its black-tipped tail.

Prime deer meat, properly and promptly looked after, is a delicious fine-grained meat highly appreciated by the backwoods people, even though the city housewife often condemns the sour, gamy taste of deer meat.

An experienced woodsman chooses his deer as carefully as the housewife buys a roast of lamb, says John Madson in his book *The White-Tailed Deer*. I fully agree with John as I have many times seen a woodsman shoot his deer close to his cabin neglecting a trophy head for a fat young buck, doe or yearling fawn. Speed in dressing, skinning and cooling is the secret of sweet-tasting venison. No cooking method can revive the taste of venison that has not been properly cared for in the bush. It is not at all surprising that venison is not very much liked by city people, as they often carry deer on front fenders or over the hoods of cars for many hundreds of miles, exposing the deer to the heat of the sun and heat and fumes of the car engine.

HUNTING CAMP VENISON LIVER AND ONIONS

Have you ever tasted fresh liver from a newly killed deer? My good friend and hunting companion, Art Dunbar has a special recipe, and once you taste it, you won't want it any other way.

The secret, according to Art, is to sauté the liver in an iron frying pan over high heat for a short period of time, just long enough to seal in the juices without making the liver tough.

1 venison liver, sliced
3 cups water
4 tablespoons flour
½ teaspoon salt
½ cup dry red wine

¼ teaspoon pepper
4 tablespoons bacon fat
2 cups wild onions, sliced
1 can mushroom soup
1 can water

Trim and wash the liver and slice into one-quarter inch thick slices. Pour half of the boiling water over the slices, drain and pat dry. Repeat. On a platter, mix the flour, salt and pepper. Dredge the liver in the flour mixture. Over high heat, heat the bacon fat until blue smoke appears.

Add the liver and sauté on both sides until lightly browned. Remove the liver with a slotted spoon and set aside.

Add the thinly sliced onions and cook until golden brown. Be careful not to burn the onions. Lower the heat, add the mushroom soup, one can of warm water and the liver. Cover and cook for 1½ hours, making sure that the pan does not cook dry. Add one-half cup of dry red wine just before the liver is ready. Serve with mashed potatoes and melted bacon grease as gravy.

FROZEN DEER LIVER

If the hunt has been good and there is more than one deer liver and the weather is cold enough, we usually freeze one to be used in camp later. Here is the way we do it.

4 cups water	3 tablespoons salt

Put the water in a large saucepan and bring to a boil, adding the salt. Stir until the salt is dissolved. Remove from heat and cool. When the water is cold, add the whole liver and soak for 3 hours. Freeze the liver.

When the liver is to be used do not defrost, it, but slice into thin slices.

1 liver, frozen	1 teaspoon salt
4 tablespoons bacon fat	½ teaspoon pepper
1 cup flour	

Place a thick bottomed frying pan over medium heat. Add the bacon fat. Dredge the liver in a mixture of flour, salt and pepper. Pan fry in bacon fat until tender. It tastes almost like fresh liver. Serve with slices of bacon and fried potatoes for breakfast.

ROASTED MARINATED DEER

While visiting Jack and Kay Hedger, we were served roast deer. Here is how this mouth-watering dish is made.

1 5-pound venison roast,	6 slices salt pork
boned	Salt and pepper

MARINADE:

1 cup dry elderberry wine	4 slices lemon
3 cups water	2 large bay leaves
1 cup maple syrup	½ cup onion, chopped
½ teaspoon salt	½ cup cattail shoots, chopped
¼ teaspoon white pepper	¼ cup wild leeks

The roast can be either a leg or a loin, trimmed of all visible fat, boned and tied with kitchen string into a neat tight roll. Rub with salt and pepper. Place the roast in a large bowl or earthenware crock. Mix together the wine, water, maple syrup, salt, pepper, lemon slices, onion, cattail shoots and wild leeks.

Pour the marinade over the roast, place in a cold spot and cover. Let stand for 24 hours, turning the roast frequently during this period so that the marinade can penetrate the meat.

Remove roast from marinade and pat dry but save the marinade. Place a thick bottomed frying pan over high heat and melt a spoonful of butter. When the butter gives off a nutty aroma, sear the roast well on all sides to seal in the juices.

Place the roast on a rack in a shallow pan, cover with the slices of salt pork. Place in a preheated oven at 325 degrees F. Cook for 30 minutes, during which time you have strained the marinade into a saucepan and heated the marinade to just below boiling point. Pour a cup of marinade over the roast, then baste the roast frequently during the rest of the cooking period, allowing 25 to 30 minutes per pound. To make gravy, transfer the roast to a heated platter and return to oven to keep warm. Strain the drippings from the pan over a saucepan; add some more of the marinade, skim off the fat from the surface, then add a mixture of flour and cold water to thicken the gravy. Season to taste, serve separately in a gravy boat.

DEER STEW WITH WILD VEGETABLES

After a long, cold, wet day in the bush, nothing can pick you up faster than the wonderful aroma of deer meat stew slowly simmering on the camp stove. One of the best stews I have ever tasted was in a lonely trapper's cabin in northern Manitoba. Here is the recipe.

1 pound venison cut into 1-inch cubes	½ teaspoon spice bush powder
3 tablespoons flour	1 tablespoon sumac cider
1 teaspoon salt	1 wild leek
1 tablespoon bacon fat	½ cup cattail shoots, diced
2½ cups maple syrup	2 cups arrowhead tubers, cubed
2 tablespoons wild onions chopped	2 tablespoons flour
	½ cup cold water

Dredge the venison in the flour and salt. Melt the bacon fat in a Dutch oven. When the bacon fat starts to smoke, add the cubed meat and with a wooden spoon, stir the meat so that it browns on all sides. Add the maple syrup, chopped onions, spice bush powder and sumac cider. Cover tightly and simmer for 2 hours. Add water if the stew cooks dry. Remove from heat and add the whole wild leek, diced cattail shoots and arrowhead tubers. Return to the heat and simmer until the vegetables are tender, about 20 minutes.

Transfer the meat and vegetables with a slotted spoon to a serving dish and put in the oven to keep warm. Thicken the juices with the flour and water to a smooth paste, stirring constantly. Pour the thickened gravy over the meat and vegetables.

ROSE FREE'S TEA BISCUITS

It took me many years before I found biscuits to do justice to this wonderful stew. When we moved to our farm, our next door neighbors Mr. and Mrs. Raymond Free arrived one day with a batch of hot home-made tea biscuits. These are guaranteed to enhance any menu.

2 cups all-purpose flour	½ cup shortening
1 tablespoon sugar	1 egg, beaten
4 tablespoons baking powder	(save 2 teaspoons)
½ teaspoon salt	2/3 cup milk

Sift together the flour, sugar, baking powder and salt. Cut in the shortening until the mixture is coarse and crumbly. Combine the milk and egg (save two teaspoons of the egg) and add to the flour mixture all at once. Stir until dough follows the fork around the bowl. Turn out on a lightly floured board.

Knead gently with the heel of your hand about twenty times. Roll dough to a three-quarter inch thickness. Cut out with a two inch floured biscuit cutter. It is important that the cutter go in the dough straight down without twisting. Place on a lightly greased cookie sheet. Brush the tops with the remainder of the egg and bake at 450 degrees F. for 10 to 14 minutes.

Serve hot with butter. These biscuits go together beautifully with the deer meat stew.

MUSTARD DEER SPARERIBS

This recipe was one of my father's favorite dishes and he never neglected to make it when he had a freshly-killed deer.

3 pounds deer ribs, trimmed and cut into 4-inch lengths	**½ cup dry red wine**
1 tablespoon salt	**2 small onions, peeled**
½ teaspoon pepper	**2 sweet bay leaves**
4 cups water	**5 whole white peppercorns**

Soak ribs in salted water overnight. Drain and pat dry with paper towels. Place the ribs in a soup kettle and add the salt, pepper, wine, onions, sweet bay leaves and whole pepper.

Bring to a boil and remove all the scum that rises to the surface. Lower heat and simmer for one hour. Remove from heat and drain on paper towels.

MUSTARD PASTE FOR COATING

½ cup white sugar	**2 tablespoons cream**
½ cup dry mustard	**2 tablespoons rum**

Mix the sugar and mustard in a small bowl. Add cream and rum to the mixture. Stir to a smooth paste and let stand for one hour.

When the ribs are cold, use a pastry brush and brush both sides of the ribs with the mustard mixture. Put the ribs on a rack in a shallow roasting pan and broil for 5 minutes on each side, making sure that the ribs are not too close to the broiler, or the mustard will burn.

The best distance from the broiler is six to eight inches. Separate the ribs with a sharp knife and serve cold as a buffet dish.

ELK (WAPITI)

When the white man first come to this continent, he encountered a large, majestic deer that to him looked like the European elk so he gave it the same name. But as we all know, the European elk is not of the moose family. The Shawnee Indians had a name for this beautiful animal, "Wapiti" and the name comes from *wab* meaning white and *atic* meaning deer. The reference to white comes from his bleached winter coat. In early spring the elk is almost white. Many names have been given to this animal; Canada stag, gray moose, to name but two.

Growing settlements and increased land clearing quickly reduced the wapiti population and the animals had to take refuge in remote areas. Today the wapiti is found on the northwest coastal slopes that merge into the great rain forests beside the Pacific.

Another region known for its herds of wapiti is the wild country in the high Rockies from southern New Mexico to northern Montana, Idaho and up through the Canadian Rockies.

The wapiti is our second largest deer, surpassed only by the moose in weight and size. It measures six to eight feet from nose to tail and stands about five feet at the shoulder. The average weight of a full grown wapiti is about 700 pounds. I have seen one as much as 1,100 pounds but this was an exceptionally large Rocky Mountain bull.

Unlike all other American deer, the elk has a pair of strange canine teeth in the forward part of the upper jaw. They are the famous 'elk teeth" sported by both bulls and cows.

These teeth were considered lucky by several Indian Tribes and were strung on thongs and worn as ornaments.

"During the early 1900's countless wapiti were killed for the "tusks" alone. The teeth were mounted in gold caps, suspended from watch chains, and worn across the ample vests of members of the Fraternal Order of Elks," says John Madson, Assistant Director of Winchester-Western's Conservation Department.

The heavy muscle and thick hide of the wapiti combine to hold body heat long after the animal has been killed, so it is most important that the carcass be dressed and cooled immediately after killing to prevent the spoilage of meat. John Madson rightly stresses this in his book *The Elk* and if you are contemplating an elk hunt I strongly advise you to read this factual book about the wapiti before you set out. The meat of an elk is coarser than that of a deer, but the flavor is much more to my liking.

The finely-grained meat is richly marbled with fat in a young animal, but tends to be coarser in an old buck, although by proper marinating, the toughness of the coarser meat can be overcome.

ELKBURGERS

The heavy bullet had hit the shoulder blade and made quite a mess of the meat all around the wound. After dressing and cutting up the meat we had a lot of small bloody pieces of meat. As the true bushman and hunter he is, Ole Johnson vowed that no meat was to be left unused, so the smaller bits and pieces of damaged meat were soaked in salt water overnight, then put through the meat mincer with one-quarter of a pound of beef suet, to every two pounds of lean elk meat.

2 pounds elk meat, ground	2 eggs
4 slices white bread, dried	½ teaspoon salt
2 wild onions, minced	¼ teaspoon pepper
1 cup milk	

Place the elk meat in a large mixing bowl and make a well in the center of the meat. Crumble the dried white bread over the meat. Add the minced onions, milk, eggs, salt and pepper to the well. Mix thoroughly with a wooden spoon. Finish mixing with your hands until the dough is smooth and pliable.

Shape the dough into patties about three inches in diameter. Place the bacon fat in a heavy frying pan and heat until a haze rises over the pan, add the patties to the pan and fry on both sides until cooked. Serve on a bed of creamed plantain leaves.

CREAMED PLANTAIN LEAVES

1 pound fresh plantain leaves	2 cups milk
2 tablespoons butter	½ teaspoon salt
2 tablespoons flour	¼ teaspoon white pepper

Clean and wash plantain leaves. Discard any discolored leaves and cut off the stalks. Place the leaves in a saucepan and cover with water. Bring to a boil, lower heat and simmer for 10 minutes. Remove from heat and drain. Pat the leaves dry with paper towels. Place the butter in another saucepan and let it melt over high heat. When it gives off a nutty aroma, add the flour stirring constantly. Add the milk and stir until you have a smooth creamy sauce. Add the salt and pepper. Lower the heat and cook for 15 minutes. Place the dried plantain leaves on a cutting board and chop finely.

Add the plantain leaves to the sauce and heat thoroughly. Place on individual plates and top with one or two elkburgers. Serve with cranberry jelly or whole cranberries.

ROAST SADDLE OF ELK IN WINE SAUCE

This wonderful recipe came from a small homestead in the Canadian wilderness. With about five acres of cultivated land, all the needs of the household were either grown or raised on the farm, supplemented by fruits and mushrooms picked in the surrounding forest. This farm was unique in that the only supplies that were store-bought were coffee, salt, spices and ammunition for the guns which were traded for pelts in the spring. Joe Bradford, his wife Liz and their three children had exchanged a university professor's relatively sheltered existence for that of an early settler's hard life several years before I came to know them. Both Joe and Liz were avid cooks and had many excellent recipes to offer. Here is one of my favorites.

3 cups elderberry wine	4 tablespoons lard
3 cups cold water	1 cup carrots, thinly sliced
5 whole juniper berries, 2 whole cloves and 8 whole black peppercorns, crushed with a mortar and pestle	½ cup wild onions, finely chopped
	¼ cup leeks, finely sliced, white part only
2 large sweet bay leaves	1½ cups cattail shoots, thinly sliced
1 tablespoon salt	3 tablespoons flour
5 pounds saddle of elk	½ cup heavy cream
4 ounces slab bacon, sliced ⅛ inch thick and cut into lardons ⅛ inch wide and about 10 inches long	4 fresh apples, poached
	1 cup lingonberry preserves

In a heavy four-quart enameled saucepan bring the wine, water, juniper berries, cloves, peppercorns, bay leaves and salt to a boil over high heat. Let cool to room temperature.

Place the elk saddle in a large earthenware crock and pour the above marinade over it. Marinate overnight in a cool place, turning the meat occasionally to let the marinade penetrate the meat on all sides.

The next day remove the meat and strain the marinade through a fine sieve into a three-quart saucepan and set aside. Pat the meat completely dry and lard in the following manner.

Insert the tip of the bacon lardon into the clip of a larding needle. Force it through the roast by pushing the point of the needle into the surface of the meat at an angle toward the backbone. Pull the needle through and trim the ends of the lardon so that half an inch protrudes from each end of the stitch. Space the lardons about one inch apart in two horizontal rows along both sides of the saddle.

Preheat the oven to 350 degrees F. In a roasting pan melt the lard over high heat until it splutters. Add the saddle and brown it on all sides, making sure that the meat browns evenly without burning. Remove to a platter, and add the carrots, wild onions, leeks and cattail shoots. Cook over moderate heat for 8 minutes, or until the vegetables are soft and lightly colored. Sprinkle the flour over the vegetables and cook over low heat for an additional 5 minutes stirring constantly to prevent the vegetables and flour from sticking to the bottom of the pan.

Arrange the vegetables in the center of the pan and put the roast on top of them. Pour in strained marinade to a depth of two inches. Roast uncovered, in the middle of the oven for 2 hours or until the meat is tender, basting with a bulb baster occasionally. Add more marinade if the liquid in the pan cooks away.

Transfer the elk saddle to a heated platter and let it rest for 10 minutes to make carving easier.

Strain the liquid in the roasting pan through a fine sieve into a small skillet, extracting all the juices from the vegetables by pressing down on them with the back of a wooden spoon. Skim the surface of the fat. You should have about three cups of liquid left. If not, add some more of the strained marinade to make this amount. Bring to a boil and add the heavy cream, beating with a wire whisk. Reduce heat and simmer for 5 minutes. Season to taste.

Serve the gravy separately. Place the roast in the middle of a platter and surround it with poached apple halves filled with lingonberry or cranberry jelly. Serve with butter-steamed new potatoes or arrowhead tubers.

BUTTER-STEAMED NEW POTATOES

25-30 small new potatoes	¼ teaspoon white pepper
8 tablespoons butter	4 tablespoons fresh dill,
1 teaspoon salt	finely chopped

Wash and scrub the potatoes under cold running water. Place on a drainboard and let drip dry. Melt the butter in a glass fireproof casserole with a cover. Add the potatoes and sprinkle them with salt, pepper and dill.

Coat the potatoes with butter by rolling them around in the casserole.

Cover with a lid that will seal the casserole completely so that no steam escapes. If the lid does not seal completely, cover the casserole with a double layer of aluminum foil, with the edges tightly folded down over the sides. Place the casserole in a low oven at 325 degrees F. for 45 minutes shaking the casserole occasionally.

Place the potatoes in a deep serving dish and sprinkle with more dill.

ELK STEAK IN WINE SAUCE

This simple but nevertheless delicious recipe for elk steaks comes from a northern Manitoba homestead and is based on an old recipe that has been in the family for many years.

3 pounds boneless elk steak
¼ cup flour
½ teaspoon salt
¼ teaspoon white pepper
½ cup butter
4 wild onions, finely chopped

2 cups puff ball mushroom
   buttons, sliced
½ cup butter
½ cup wild leeks, white parts
   only, finely chopped
1 cup dry elderberry wine

Trim fat from the steaks and wipe well with a damp cloth. Dredge steaks in the flour, salt and pepper. Melt the butter in a heavy iron frying pan over high heat until the butter gives off a nutty aroma.

Add the steaks, one at a time and brown on both sides. Set the steaks aside and keep warm. Add more butter and onions; cook until golden brown. Remove the onions with a slotted spoon and set aside. Add the puff ball mushrooms to the pan and sauté until tender. Return the steaks and onions to the frying pan with half a cup of butter. Cover the pan and simmer for 25 minutes or until the steaks are tender. Add the elderberry wine and simmer for not more than 5 minutes.

Transfer the steaks to a serving platter and top with onion-mushroom mixture. Serve with beans, peas and potatoes.

GROUNDHOG OR WOODCHUCK

This heavy-set rodent is the largest member of the squirrel family. He is a familiar sight in rural areas as a game animal for small-bore rifle hunting and is considered a pest when he moves into gardens. Unfortunately most people do not consider him edible and for this reason they leave him in the fields after the kill. The groundhog feeds exclusively on fresh green vegetation, including clover and alfalfa, and will eat garden vegetables as well as wild plants.

You will find this rodent in farmers' fields, pastures, ravines, woodlots and semi-open forests. He spends the daylight hours feeding or sunning himself on a rock or other vantage point. He is extremely shy and often long range shots are used to kill him.

The best time of the year to eat groundhog meat is in the fall when he is enormously fat before he enters his hibernating chamber.

The meat is dark and fine-grained and not unlike the beaver in taste. As the woodchuck is not a large animal, the meat is usually used in stews and meat pies.

GROUNDHOG MEAT AND VEGETABLE CASSEROLE

While visiting a friend who had just taken over an old homestead, I was invited to go on a groundhog hunt, as his fields were full of groundhog holes which were a menace to his livestock. We set out early in the morning and it wasn't long before we had fifteen well-fed groundhogs bagged. He surprised me by suggesting that we skin them and bring them back to the farm. In his woodshed he already had a dozen or more skinned groundhogs. I couldn't contain my curiosity any longer and asked him what in the world he was going to do with all the groundhogs. He explained that groundhog meat was very tasty in a stew or casserole, a lesson he had learned from an old farmer many years ago.

He selected a well hung carcass to have for supper that night and set out to prove to me how tasty a meal could be made of this rodent. When it was ready, I approached it with some reluctance and scepticism. To my surprise the dinner was delicious, and here is the recipe.

2 pounds woodchuck meat, parboiled
½ cup salt pork, cubed
1 clove garlic
2 cups potatoes, diced
1 cup wild onions, minced
2 cups water
1 bay leaf

1 cup tart apple juice
8 peppercorns, whole
1 teaspoon salt
4 tablespoons bacon fat
4 tablespoons flour
1 cup heavy cream

Wipe the woodchuck dry, cut it into two pieces and place it in a large soup kettle. Cover with water, then add the cubed salt pork and garlic cloves. Bring quickly to a boil, lower the heat and simmer for 1½ hours, skimming the scum as it rises to the surface. Remove from heat and let stand in the cooking juices until room temperature. Remove the meat and with a sharp knife cut all the meat from the bones. Discard the bones and set the meat aside. Melt some bacon fat in a two-quart casserole and add meat. Top with diced potatoes and sprinkle with the minced onions.

In a heavy frying pan add the water, bay leaf, apple juice, peppercorns and salt. Bring to a boil, remove from heat and strain through a fine sieve and set aside. Melt the bacon fat over high heat and add the flour stirring constantly. Add the cream slowly to make a smooth sauce. Add the strained juice to the cream-bacon mixture using a wire whisk to make it smooth. Let it simmer for 10 minutes, then add to the meat and vegetable casserole. Bake in a slow oven (325 degrees F. for one hour). Serve with cooked rice and currant jelly.

BRAISED GROUNDHOG IN SPICED RED WINE SAUCE

Here is another groundhog recipe from the same friend, this time with a wine sauce.

½ pound lean bacon; finely chopped
1 5-pound groundhog, cut into
serving pieces or use 2, 3-pound
groundhogs, cut into serving pieces
½ teaspoon salt
½ teaspoon black pepper
½ cup flour
½ cup wild onion, finely chopped

½ teaspoon garlic, finely chopped
1 cup dry red wine
1 cup chicken stock
2 tablespoons brandy
1 teaspoon red currant jelly
1 bay leaf
¼ teaspoon dried rosemary
¼ teaspoon dried thyme

In a heavy flameproof five-quart casserole, cook the bacon over moderate heat until crisp. Drain the bacon and set the casserole aside.

Wash the groundhog quickly under cold running water and pat dry with paper towels. Sprinkle the pieces with salt and pepper and then dip them in flour, shaking off any excess flour. Heat the casserole until the fat splutters.

Add the floured groundhog pieces a few at a time and brown them evenly on all sides. As they are done, transfer the groundhog pieces to a plate. Pour off. all but two tablespoons of fat from the casserole and in it cook the onions and garlic, stirring frequently, for 6 to 7 minutes. Pour in the wine and chicken stock and bring to a boil over high heat, scraping off any brown bits stuck to the bottom of the casserole. Stir in the brandy, currant jelly, bay leaf, rosemary and thyme. Return the pieces of groundhog to the casserole; add the drained bacon, cover the casserole tightly and simmer over low heat for 2 hours or until the meat is tender but not falling apart. Pick out the bay leaf and taste for seasoning. The dish should be quite peppery.

Serve the groundhog directly from the casserole.

WOODCHUCK STEW WITH SOUR CREAM

After having been converted to woodchuck meat, I made this stew from a generations old Swedish recipe.

2 tablespoons butter
2 tablespoons vegetable oil
2 pounds woodchuck meat, parboiled,
boned and cut into 1 inch cubes
1 large wild onion, thinly sliced
1 tablespoon flour

½ teaspoon salt
¼ teaspoon spice bush powder
½ teaspoon black pepper
1 bay leaf
1½ cups beef stock
3 tablespoons sour cream

Cut the woodchuck in half, wash under cold running water and wipe dry with a damp cloth. Put into a soup kettle, cover with water and bring to a boil. Remove all the scum as it rises to the surface. Lower the heat and simmer for 30 minutes. Remove from the heat and drain off all the cooking juices. Let stand in the cooking juices until it reaches room temperature. When cool, cut out all the bones, dice the meat into one-inch cubes and set aside.

Preheat the oven to 350 degrees F. Heat the butter and oil in a heavy skillet. Add the meat and brown well on all sides. Transfer the meat to a four-quart casserole with a cover. Replace the skillet over the heat and add the onion. Cook until the onion is golden brown and transparent. Add the onions to the casserole, making sure that all the pieces from the skillet are added to the casserole. Toss lightly and sprinkle the flour over the top. Add the salt, pepper, spice bush powder and bay leaf.

Pour the beef stock over the casserole and cook in the oven for 2 hours, or until the meat is tender. Transfer the meat to a heated platter and cover lightly with foil.

With a large spoon, remove all the fat from the surface of the casserole and discard it. With a wire whisk, beat in the sour cream one tablespoon at a time. Taste for seasoning and add salt and pepper if necessary. Pour the sauce over the meat and serve hot with potatoes and vegetables.

SWEET PICKLED WOODCHUCK

This recipe comes out of a handwritten cookbook dating from about the early 1800's. Small changes had to be made to convert old weights and measures into modern ones.

1 groundhog, skinned and cleaned	1 teaspoon cinnamon
½ cup vinegar	½ teaspoon ground cloves
1 teaspoon salt	½ cup brown sugar
2 tablespoons soda	½ cup apple cider
2 tablespoons dry mustard	½ cup maple syrup
3 tablespoons mixed pickling spice	Grated rind of one lemon

Wash groundhog thoroughly with salt and water, then let soak overnight covered in cold water. Add vinegar and one tablespoon salt to the water. The next morning, remove the groundhog from the brine, wash under running cold water and put in a soup kettle. Cover the groundhog with a solution of two tablespoons soda and two quarts of water. Bring to a boil over high heat and boil for 20 minutes, removing all scum that rises to the surface. Drain and rinse the meat and place the groundhog in a clean pot. Tie all the pickling spices in a cheesecloth and put on the meat. Add water just to cover. Bring to a boil, lower heat and simmer for 35 minutes.

Drain and rinse the groundhog meat, pat dry and transfer to rack in a roasting pan. In a bowl, mix the sugar, mustard, apple cider and maple syrup to a thin paste. With a brush cover the meat with the mixture and cook in the oven at 325 degrees F., basting occasionally with the remaining mustard mixture for 1½ hours or until meat is tender. Remove from the oven, cut into serving pieces and serve from a heated platter with scalloped potatoes.

GROUNDHOG IN SOUR CREAM

A delightful way to convince non-believers that this meat is delicious.

1 groundhog, skinned and cleaned	1 teaspoon salt
½ cup vinegar	½ teaspoon allspice
1 tablespoon salt	½ cup bacon fat
2 quarts water	3 wild onions
2 teaspoons soda	½ cup water
½ cup flour	1 cup sour cream

Wash and dry the groundhog and put it in an earthenware crock. Cover with water and add half a cup of vinegar and one tablespoon salt. Let stand in a cool place overnight. In the morning remove from brine, wash and pat dry with a damp cloth. In a large soup kettle combine two quarts of water and two tablespoons of soda. Bring to a boil, lower the heat and simmer for 15 minutes, removing scum as it rises to the surface. Drain and rinse the groundhog meat and cut into serving pieces. Combine the flour, salt and allspice and dredge the pieces of meat in the mixture. Preheat oven to 325 degrees F. Melt the bacon fat in a heavy iron frying pan until smoking. Brown meat on all sides. Transfer the browned meat into a greased four-quart casserole. Arrange sliced onions on top, add the water, cover and bake in pre-heated oven for 2 hours or until meat is tender. Transfer meat to a heated platter to keep warm. Put the casserole on top of the stove over medium heat and spoon in the sour cream stirring constantly.

Don't let the sauce come to a boil. Place the meat back into the casserole and simmer for about 15 minutes.

Serve with creamed dandelion leaves.

CREAMED DANDELION LEAVES

1 pound of fresh young dandelion leaves	2 tablespoons butter 2 tablespoons flour
1 quart water	1 cup milk
½ teaspoon salt	Salt and pepper

Clean and wash the dandelion leaves and place in a three-quart saucepan. Add the water and salt; let come to a boil. Lower heat and simmer for 15 minutes. Remove from heat and drain in a colander.

Over high heat melt the butter in a two-quart saucepan, add the flour and work mixture into a smooth paste. Add the milk to make a smooth thick cream. Add the salt and pepper to taste.

Place the dandelion leaves, well drained on a cutting board and chop finely. Add the dandelion leaves to the sauce and mix well, reheating if necessary. Serve with the groundhog meat in a large bowl.

MOOSE

Moose is the world's largest living deer. This majestic wood dweller is the king of the forest and its range extends from Nova Scotia and New Brunswick to northern Alaska.

In appearance the bull moose is dominated by his antlers, which are flat and broad, spreading widely with upcurved sweeping sections and many points. It is quite startling that in spite of his size and awkward appearance he moves swiftly and almost soundlessly through the bush.

As befits a true king of the forest, he lives a solitary life and is seldom found in larger than family groups.

In addition to their basic diet of broad-leafed trees and shrubs, moose seek out aquatic vegetation during the summer months. This is the time of year when they can be sighted along rivers and lakesides almost completely submerged as they dive for tender aquatic plants growing on lake bottoms.

In the fall their mating calls are heard, sounding like blasts from a diesel horn. A friend of mine who is an engineer with Ontario Northern Railways says that he has often seen great bull moose challenging diesel locomotives because of the similar sound of their horns.

Every year thousands of hunters enter in pursuit of this giant of the wilderness who can weigh in at 1,800 pounds. Normally the moose does not make unprovoked attacks on people. A cow may defend her calf, but it is more likely to run away with it if startled.

The bull, except during the rut, seems to be more curious than alarmed or angry if approached within a reasonable distance. If seriously bothered, bulls may chase people up into trees and keep them there for hours. Sometimes they may even patrol the door of a cabin, making its occupant a prisoner.

The moose is a highly sought-after game meat. It used to be one of the staple foods for northern trappers and settlers. Indians often hunted this animal with bow and arrow or with dead-fall snares.

JELLIED MOOSE NOSE

During one of my first hunting trips to northern Ontario, I was invited to accompany Indian Joe on a moose hunt. I arrived at his cabin late in the afternoon just before supper and was treated to this delicacy. Indian Joe served me with this dish to hone my hunting instinct for the next morning's hunt, because he said that if you have this dish once you will want it again.

Here is the way he prepared this delicacy.

1 upper jawbone of moose	1 teaspoon salt
2 wild onions	1 teaspoon pepper
1 tablespoon spice bush powder	½ cup Indian vinegar

After having cut the upper jawbone of the moose just below the eyes, he put it in a large soup kettle filled with boiling water for one hour. Then the jaw was plunged into a pot filled with ice-cold water. When well chilled, the hairs were removed. The cooking beforehand makes this task quite easy. Wash thoroughly until all hairs are removed. Put in a soup kettle and cover with water. Add the sliced onions, spice powder and vinegar, bring to a boil, then reduce heat and simmer until meat is tender.

Let cool in the kettle overnight. The next morning, take the meat out of the broth. Remove the bones and cartilage and discard them. The nose contains two kinds of meat, white meat from the bulb of the nose, and thin strips of dark meat from along the bones. Slice the meat thinly and alternate layers of white and dark meat in a loaf pan. Boil down the broth by about two-thirds. Pour the remaining broth over the meat and store in a cool place until jellied. Slice and serve cold.

STUFFED MOOSE HEART

Moose heart and liver are without equal for tenderness and flavor. Hence it is important that these organs be well cared for as soon as possible after the kill.

As it is often a tiresome job to backpack 1,000 pounds of moose meat, the liver and heart should be the first to be brought out and cooked. My father prepared the heart this way.

1 moose heart	4 tablespoons butter
2 quarts cold water	1 small onion, chopped
1 tablespoon salt	½ teaspoon sage
1 cup fine bread crumbs	¼ teaspoon pepper
1 cup tart apples, minced	Flour, salt and pepper for
½ teaspoon salt	dredging the heart

Bring to a boil two quarts of water and one tablespoon salt. Remove from heat and cool. When cold, wipe the heart with a damp cloth and soak in the brine overnight.

Mix the bread crumbs, apples, salt, melted butter, onion, sage and pepper. Drain the heart, hollow out the top and stuff loosely with the stuffing.

Using a needle and thread, sew the heart together. Dredge the heart in a mixture of the flour, salt and pepper. Preheat the oven to 325 degrees F.

Bake in a covered roaster for 3 hours or until tender. Baste occasionally to keep the surface tender and moist. Serve with potatoes and green vegetables.

MOOSE LIVER AND WILD RICE CASSEROLE

This recipe is ideal for hunting camp cooking because it can be cooking while you are out hunting.

4 cups boiling water, salted	½ cup raisins
1 cup wild rice	2 tablespoons maple syrup
3 tablespoons butter	2 teaspoons salt
1 wild onion, finely chopped	¼ teaspoon pepper
2 cups milk	¼ teaspoon allspice
2 eggs, lightly beaten	1½ pounds moose liver,
¼ cup cooked and crumbled	finely chopped
lean bacon	

Cook the wild rice in four cups of briskly boiling salted water for 20 minutes. Drain the rice through a fine sieve and set aside. In a heavy iron frying pan, melt two tablespoons of butter over moderate heat. When the foam subsides, add the onion and cook for 8 minutes, or until golden brown and transparent. Remove from heat and set aside. Preheat the oven to 350 degrees F.

In a large mixing bowl, gently combine the wild rice, milk and lightly beaten eggs. Add the cooked onions, crumbled bacon, raisins and maple syrup. Season with the salt, pepper and allspice. Stir in the finely chopped liver and mix thoroughly.

Grease a two-quart casserole or baking dish with the rest of the butter and pour in the liver-rice mixture. Bake uncovered in the middle of the oven for 2 hours, or until a knife inserted in the center of the casserole comes out clean. Serve hot with cranberry sauce.

MOOSE LIVER WITH WILD APPLES AND ONION RINGS

Often in the moose hunting season you can be lucky and find a wild apple tree still full of fruit. A delightful dish can be created by using these usually tart apples with onions and a moose liver.

1 cup butter	1 teaspoon salt
4 wild onions, cut into	½ teaspoon pepper
thin slices and separated	10 wild apples
into rings	2 pounds moose liver, cut into
½ cup flour	¼ inch slices

Preheat the oven to 250 degrees F. In a heavy skillet, melt four tablespoons of butter over moderate heat. Add the onion rings, half of the salt, and pepper. Stirring occasionally, cook the rings to a golden brown, approximately 10 minutes. With a slotted spoon, transfer to a heatproof plate; cover with aluminum foil and put in heated oven. Add four tablespoons butter to the skillet and drop the peeled, cored and crosswise sliced apples into the skillet. Cook until golden on both sides. Remove from the skillet and put in the oven with the onion rings. Season the liver with the rest of the salt and pepper and dip the slices in the flour. Add the remaining butter to the skillet and melt over medium heat. When the foam subsides, add the liver and cook for 3 minutes on each side, or until the slices are light brown. Transfer liver to a heated platter, top with apples and onion rings and serve at once.

ROULADES OF MOOSE STUFFED WITH ANCHOVIES AND ONIONS

This recipe comes from my father's recipe book and has been in our family for a hundred years or more. Lean moose meat is ideal for this dish.

2 pounds moose round steak	1 teaspoon salt
8 tablespoons butter	½ teaspoon pepper
1 cup wild onions, finely chopped	16 flat anchovy fillets
2 tablespoons flour	½ cup beef stock

Cut eight pieces, six by three inches and about one inch thick from the round roast; pound the meat with a meat pounder to a thickness of about one-eighth of an inch.

Heat three tablespoons butter in a heavy iron frying pan. Add the chopped wild onion and cook for 8 minutes, or until golden brown but not burned. Remove from heat and stir in the flour. Return to heat and cook for 5 minutes stirring constantly. Reserve two tablespoons of the roux for the sauce.

Sprinkle the salt and pepper over the meat and spread the roux evenly over it. Lay two anchovy fillets on each slice, roll up securely and tie with a loop of kitchen string at each end of the roll.

Heat the rest of the butter in the frying pan. When the foam subsides, add the roulades one at a time and brown on all sides. Arrange the browned roulades in a single layer in a three-quart casserole or baking dish with a cover.

Preheat oven to 350 degrees F. De-glaze the frying pan by pouring one-half cup of beef stock into the pan. Let boil for 2 minutes, stirring to scrape up any bits clinging to the pan. Add two tablespoons of the roux that you have kept for this purpose, and cook over medium heat for 3 to 4 minutes, stirring briskly, until the sauce thickens. Pour sauce over roulades, cover and bake for 45 minutes. Serve with mashed potatoes and lingonberries.

ROYAL MOOSE ROAST

Here is a royal dish from a royal animal. Glazed new potatoes and caramelled carrots go well with it.

3 cups elderberry wine	2 tablespoons Indian vinegar
3 cups cold water	2 cups beef stock
1 large bay leaf	1 large bay leaf
1 tablespoon salt	4 slices goat cheese
5 pounds moose round steak	1 tablespoon peppercorns,
4 ounces slab bacon	crushed
1 cup wild onions, finely chopped	1 teaspoon salt
2 tablespoons maple syrup	½ teaspoon pepper

Slice the bacon into one-eighth of an inch thick slices and cut into lardons one-eighth of an inch wide and about ten inches long. Store in the refrigerator.

In a large soup kettle, bring the wine, water, bay leaf and salt to a boil over high heat. Let marinade cool to room temperature. Place the moose meat in a large earthenware crock and pour the marinade over the meat. Turn the roast to moisten it thoroughly on all sides. Marinate for 24 hours in a cool place, turning the meat several times. Remove meat from the marinade and pat dry. Lard the roast in the following manner.

Insert the larding needle with the lardon securely fastened by the clip and push the needle through the roast. Trim the ends of the lardon so that one-half inch protrudes from each end of the stitch. Space the lardons about an inch apart and in two horizontal rows. Preheat the oven to 350 degrees F.

Place a large iron pot with a lid on the top of stove over high heat. Melt the butter in it. When the butter gives off a nutty aroma, add the meat and brown on all sides for at least 15 minutes. Remove the meat from the pot and set aside. Add the chopped onions to the pot and cook for 10 minutes, or until they are golden brown. Remove the pot from heat and add the flour. Stir gently to dissolve it, then pour in the maple syrup, Indian vinegar and beef stock. Add the bay leaf, goat cheese and crushed peppercorns.

Add the meat to the pot, cover and bring to a boil on top of the stove. Place in a preheated oven and simmer for 3 hours, basting the meat occasionally with a bulb baster.

Transfer roast to a heated platter and keep warm in the turned-off oven. Remove the bay leaf and peppercorns and discard them. Skim off any surface fat and season to taste. Serve gravy separately. Accompany with lingonberries or red currant jelly.

MARINATED PAN-BROILED MOOSE STEAKS

If the temptation to use freshly-killed meat is too strong to resist, here is a way to speed up the aging process of moose meat.

¼ cup vinegar	¼ teaspoon pepper
2 tablespoons water	½ teaspoon paprika
¼ cup salad oil	¼ teaspoon garlic salt
1 teaspoon salt	6 moose steaks 1¼-inches thick
½ teaspoon dry mustard	½ teaspoon salt
1 tablespoon grated wild onion	¼ teaspoon pepper
2 tablespoons maple syrup	1 teaspoon charcoal salt

Pound the steaks with a meat mallet, or with the broad side of a heavy knife. After pounding, the steaks should be about three-quarters of an inch thick. Combine the vinegar, two tablespoons water, salad oil, dry mustard, onion, maple syrup and pepper in a large earthenware crock. Mix well and add the steaks to the marinade.

Marinate in a cool place for 48 hours. Remove the steaks from the marinade and drain. Pat dry with a damp cloth. Mix the salt, pepper and charcoal salt and rub the steaks with the mixture. Place a heavy iron frying pan on top of the stove over light heat and rub the frying pan with a piece of salt pork just enough to prevent the steaks from sticking to the bottom of the pan. Cook the steaks quickly over high heat turning every minute until the steaks are done. It is important not to overcook them. Serve with pan-fried potatoes.

WILD GAME MARINADE

Often the same marinade can be used for all large and small game. I give here the marinade I usually use for my large game with variations that I found to be necessary for differences in taste for the different meats. Usually older, large game require more time in the marinade to break down the fibers and to make the meat tender and tasty.

However, no marinade in the world can take the place of a long hanging period. Here is my recipe for marinade.

1 quart dry red wine	1 teaspoon pepper
2 cups vinegar	2 bay leaves
2 cups wild grape juice	½ teaspoon cinnamon
2 onions, finely chopped	¼ teaspoon thyme
2 teaspoons salt	4 whole cloves

For best results, place all the ingredients in a large soup kettle and bring to a boil over high heat. Remove from heat and cool to room temperature before adding the meat. I usually marinate my game from one to four days before cooking. It is very important that the vessel in which the marinade is kept be either stainless steel or earthenware. Earthenware is best.

MOOSE MINCE MEAT

My grandmother Bolsby always used this recipe. It was given to my grandmother at the time of her marriage in 1895. As was then the custom, a bride-to-be was given recipes at a homesteading bee, a forerunner to today's shower. My mother has used this recipe all her married life and according to my husband there isn't a tastier mince meat pie recipe in existence. It calls for stewing beef but we have used moose meat many times with wonderful results. The amounts given here yield sixteen pints of mince meat. I usually store the mince meat in sterilized pint sealers. As an ordinary pie uses one pint, we have mince meat pie filling for a long time.

3 pounds moose stewing beef	4 cups dark brown sugar
1 pound beef suet	6 teaspoons salt
2 pounds seedless raisins	6 teaspoons ground cinnamon
2 pounds seeded raisins	6 teaspoons ground cloves
1 pound currants	6 teaspoons ground allspice
½ pound mixed peel (including citron)	6 teaspoons ground nutmeg
½ pound blanched almonds (break	6 pounds tart apples, peeled
the almonds up with your fingers	1 quart apple cider
not with a knife)	

Wash and pat the stewing beef dry. Place in a large kettle, cover with water and bring to a boil. Lower heat and simmer for 2 hours, removing all the scum as it rises to the surface. When well cooked, remove from heat and cool. Remove all fat and gristle from the meat.

Put the meat, suet and apples through a meat grinder using the medium knife. Grind into a large bowl and make sure that all the juices are collected. Place the meat, juices and apples in a large earthenware crock, add the raisins, currants, mixed peel, almonds, brown sugar and spices and mix thoroughly, adding the apple cider to keep the mixture moist. Let stand overnight in a cool place, stirring frequently during this time. If the mixture seems too dry, add more apple cider.

Place in sterilized pint sealers and store in a cool place.

JENNIE PAULL'S SPICED BEEF

Here is another recipe where beef can be substituted for moose meat and makes a wonderful dish for the buffet table. The meat is served thinly sliced and cold.

1 8-pound round roast of moose	4½ tablespoons ground pepper
1 cup dark brown sugar	2 tablespoons ground cloves
2 tablespoons saltpeter	1 tablespoon salt
4 tablespoons ground allspice	1 tablespoon dry mustard

Mix the sugar, saltpeter, allspice, pepper, cloves and mustard and set aside. Wipe the roast well with a damp cloth. Rub in as much of the sugar-spice mixture into the roast as you can. Place the roast in an earthenware crock and sprinkle with the rest of the spices. Cover loosely and store in a cool place. Then, every day for the next 3 weeks, turn the roast over in the juices that have formed in the crock. The first week it is advisable to turn the roast twice a day.

After three weeks in the marinade, transfer the roast to a large enamel kettle and cover with lukewarm water. Bring the water to a boil, lower heat to a slow simmer and cover. Simmer for 2 hours or until the roast is fork tender. Remove and cool. Slice in thin slices.

MUSKRAT

The muskrat is the largest of the family *Cricetidae*. It is easily recognized not only by size but by its tail, which is laterally compressed, scaly and covered with sparse hairs.

The muskrat ranges practically all over North America. However, it is not found in the southeastern United States, southern North Carolina, south-central Texas or southern California. The muskrat inhabits ponds, streams and marshes.

Since early Indian days, the muskrat has been valuable to man. Its flesh is sweet and tender, its fur is warm and durable. From its tail the Indians drew long fine sinews which were used as fish lines or as thread to sew fur coats or moccassins together.

Today the muskrat is more valuable than ever. In many states it ranks first as a fur-bearer, both in quality and quantity available. Since the word 'muskrat' is such an ugly name for a beautiful fur, most dyed pelts are marketed as Hudson seal.

Similarly, muskrat is not a very pleasant name for a table dish. No one relishes the idea of eating "rat" meat, although the muskrat is no more related to Old World rats than dogs are to cats. "March rabbit" or "Maryland terrapin" are much more delectable names for muskrat steak. In addition to being valuable as a food and fur bearer, the muskrat is important in its own right in relation to the other forms of life that comprise its habitat. For instance, muskrat eating houses and haycock houses offer readymade platforms for nesting ducks and other marsh birds.

In the marshes, streams and ponds, where redwings nest, and other marshland habitants busy themselves with the important business of living, the muskrat builds channels, haycock homes, eating huts, rears its young, feeds and is fed upon as a part of the natural balance of life in his watery realm.

When cleaning the muskrat for eating purposes, it is important to remove the two musk glands that are located at the base of the tail. After removing the glands, make sure that the skinning knife is well cleaned before it is used again.

MUSKRAT MEAT PATTIES

Many a time when I am in a position to obtain muskrat, I make meat patties out of the meat, but to make this dish you have to have a meat grinder handy.

2 medium muskrats, cleaned and boned	**1 egg, well beaten**
½ pound salt pork	**1 teaspoon salt**
2 wild onions, finely chopped	**½ teaspoon pepper**
2 wild leeks, finely chopped	**4 tablespoons butter**
3 tablespoons flour	**2 tablespoons vegetable oil**
1½ cups club soda	

Put the muskrat meat, salt pork, onion and leeks through the meat grinder twice, using the finest blade.

In a large mixing bowl, vigorously beat the flour into the ground meat mixture with a wooden spoon. Gradually beat in the club soda, a few tablespoons at a time. Continue to beat until the meat is light and fluffy. Beat in the egg, salt and pepper. Cover the bowl with aluminum foil and keep in a cool place for an hour. This will make the meat mixture much easier to handle. Shape it into round meat patties about three-inches in diameter and about one-inch thick.

Melt the butter and oil in an iron frying pan over high heat. When the foam subsides, lower the heat to moderate and add the meat patties, a few at a time, taking care not to crowd them. Cook for 10 minutes on each side, turning the patties with a large spoon or spatula so that they won't break. When the patties are a dark golden brown, transfer to a heated platter. Continue until all are ready. As the patties contain pork, make sure that they are cooked throughout. Test with tip of a knife in the middle of one patty; if no pink juice emerges, it is cooked. Serve with boiled potatoes and pickled beets.

MUSKRAT MEAT LOAF IN SOUR CREAM PASTRY

Hungry and tired, I arrived at a trapper friend's door, late one winter evening. I was met by a wonderful aroma drifting from the stove. "You are just in time to join me for dinner", I was told and I sat down to a meal I will long remember. After the meal, enjoying our black coffee and our pipes, I asked him for the recipe. Here it is.

PASTRY:

2¼ cups flour	1 egg
1 teaspoon salt	½ cup sour cream
12 tablespoons chilled butter	or yogurt
cut into ¼-inch pieces	1 tablespoon soft butter

Sift the flour and salt into a large chilled bowl. Drop the butter pieces into the bowl. Working quickly and using your fingertips mix the flour and butter together until they resemble coarse meal. In a separate bowl, combine the egg and sour cream, and add the flour-butter mixture, working with your fingers until the dough is soft and pliable. Wrap in wax paper and chill for one hour. Cut the chilled dough in half and roll out each half on a floured board. Butter the bottom of a jelly-roll pan with the soft butter, lift one of the sheets of dough over the rolling pin and line the bottom of the pan. Set aside.

MUSKRAT MEAT FILLING

8 tablespoons butter	¼ cup mint, finely chopped
¾ cup mushrooms, finely chopped	1 cup grated cheddar cheese
4 cups cooked muskrat meat,	½ cup milk
finely chopped	1 egg, combined with two
½ cup onions, finely chopped	tablespoons milk

Melt the butter in a heavy frying pan over high heat. When the butter gives off a nutty aroma, lower the heat and add the mushrooms. Cook over moderate heat, stirring frequently for 8 to 10 minutes. Add the cooked and chopped muskrat meat and continue to cook for 5 minutes. Scrape the meat mixture from the pan into a large mixing bowl and stir in the onions, mint, cheese and milk. Now gather this meat mixture into a ball and place it in the center of the dough in the prepared jelly pan.

With your hands, pat the meat into a narrow loaf extending across the center of the dough from one end to the other. Lift the second sheet of pastry dough over the rolling pin and drape it on top of the meat loaf.

Dip a pastry brush into the egg-milk mixture and moisten the edges of the dough. Press down with a fork to make a complete seal, all around the edges. Prick the top of the loaf in several places to allow steam to escape. Heat the oven to 375 degrees F. Brush the loaf with the egg-milk mixture and set the pan in the middle of the oven. Bake for one hour, or until the loaf turns a golden brown. Serve thick slices of the hot meat loaf, accompanied by a bowl of whole cranberries.

MUSKRAT MEAT LOAF

A couple of days later we found more muskrats in his traps, and as he was a firm believer that no meat should be wasted, all the muskrats were skinned, cleaned and frozen for future use. He said, with a glint in his eyes, "you sell the skins and eat the meat and you make twice the money."

During my stay with him, we had muskrat in one form or another every day, but I never tired of this delicious meat.

1½ pounds muskrat, ground	½ teaspoon thyme
2 eggs, beaten	1 teaspoon salt
½ cup dry bread crumbs	½ teaspoon pepper
1 cup evaporated milk	1 teaspoon Worcestershire sauce
2 wild onions, grated	½ cup catsup

Wash and clean the muskrat, making sure that the musk glands are removed. Cut meat from bones with a sharp knife, then grind the meat in a meat grinder, using medium coarse knife. In a large mixing bowl, combine the beaten eggs, breadcrumbs, milk, onion, thyme, salt and pepper. Mix well and let stand for half an hour. Add the ground meat, Worcestershire sauce and catsup. Mix with fingers until the meat mixture is moist and smooth. Preheat the oven to 350 degrees F. Grease a loaf pan and put the meat mixture in it. Place the pan in a shallow dish containing hot water and bake for 1½ hours.

Serve with potatoes and cranberries.

FRIED MUSKRAT

For people who don't like a strong gamy taste, here is a recipe which I think will suit everyone.

1 muskrat	½ cup milk
1 tablespoon salt	1 teaspoon salt
1 quart water	½ cup breadcrumbs
1 egg yolk	4 tablespoons butter

Wash and clean muskrat and wipe dry with a cloth, making sure that the musk glands are removed. Rub the salt on the meat inside and out. Place in a crock with one quart of cold water. Let stand overnight. Mix the egg and milk in a small bowl and set aside. Transfer the muskrat to a soup kettle, cover with cold water and bring to a boil over high heat. Lower heat and simmer for 30 minutes. Remove from heat and let stand until it reaches room temperature. Remove the muskrat from the juice and cut into serving pieces. Dip the pieces in the egg-milk mixture, sprinkle salt and breadcrumbs on the pieces and drain on a paper towel. Melt the butter in a very hot frying pan. Lower the heat and place the pieces of meat in the pan and brown on all sides. When all the pieces are browned, reduce heat and simmer for 2 hours, or until the meat is tender.

Serve with pan fried potatoes and cranberries.

(This method of preparing muskrat was once served by the author of *Canadian Game Cookery*, Frances MacIlquham, at a sophisticated wild game dinner for the Outdoor Writers of Canada.)

PORCUPINE

The porcupine, with its covering of 30,000 sharp quills, is undoubtedly the most distinctive rodent in North America.

The porcupine, the utmost in survival food, has saved thousands of lives in the wilderness. As a matter of fact, an unwritten law amongst woodsmen says never kill a porcupine, except in an emergency.

The porcupine is a heavily built mammal with fairly large feet with four toes on the front and five on the hindlegs. The tail is thick and heavily armed with quills. The old wives tale that the porcupine can throw its quills is completely unfounded. As the quills are equipped with tiny barbs, they are difficult and painful to remove. One way to make this easier is to cut off the protruding end and let the air out of the quill.

The porcupine is found throughout North America except in the southern part of the United States. It is active the year around and at all hours of the day or night.

The porcupine often becomes a nuisance around cabins and cottages, chewing sills, doors, tools or anything with a trace of salt in it, especially during the winter when such places are deserted. A trapper friend of mine found the solution to this nuisance; in the late fall he drilled one-inch holes in several stumps and filled the holes. Then he covered the stumps with a strong salt brine. He always emptied his curing brine during the winter over these stumps. He claims that since he started this treatment no damage has been done to his camp.

The flesh of the porcupine is fatty but delicious. It should, as a general rule, be parboiled, particularly in late winter or early spring as it tastes of the food it has eaten, usually bark from the pine or aspen tree.

MUSTARD COVERED PORCUPINE RIBS

I introduced this dish to the Outdoor Writers of Canada at their annual wild game banquet with great success, but few of these experts believed me when I told them what they had eaten.

1 large porcupine, skinned and cleaned	3 tablespoons dry mustard
	2 tablespoons brown sugar
3 quarts water	2 tablespoons heavy cream
1 tablespoon salt	3 tablespoons rye whiskey

Wash and clean the porcupine. Remove all excess fat. To a large soup kettle add three quarts of water and one tablespoon of salt. Bring to a boil over high heat. Lower the heat and add the porcupine. Simmer for 30 minutes and remove all scum that rises to the surface. Remove from heat and cool to room temperature. Place the porcupine on several layers of paper towels to drain.

Pat dry, then cut in serving pieces. Save the ribs intact, but remove all other bones.

In a small bowl, combine the dry mustard, sugar, and cream. With a rotary beater beat the mixture into a smooth paste. Add the whiskey, tablespoon by tablespoon, stirring constantly. Keep in a medium warm place for one hour. With a pastry brush, cover all the porcupine meat with a light coating of the mustard mixture and place the meat on the rack of a roasting pan.

Broil in the oven, ten inches from the broiler, for 20 minutes. Remove from pan, turn the meat over and cover the other side with the rest of the mustard mixture. Return and broil for about 15 minutes. Remove from the oven, turn the meat again and cover with a thin layer of mustard mixture. Let cool. Serve with arrowhead tubers in white sauce.

ARROWHEAD TUBERS IN WHITE SAUCE

An easy way to collect arrowhead tubers is to copy the Indians — raid the muskrat feeding houses in late fall or as soon as ice has formed on the marsh. If you are collecting the tubers from the fresh plant, remember that the tubers are not directly below the plant's leaves, but often several feet away stemming out in all directions on long runners. A pitchfork is the best tool to use. When dislodged from the runners the tubers will float to the surface and can easily be collected. Pick only the ones that you want; leave the rest to float. In a few days the tubers will sink to the bottom and form a new plant for harvesting the next fall.

1 pound medium size arrowhead tubers, washed and scraped	1½ cups milk
½ cup butter	1 teaspoon salt
½ cup flour	½ teaspoon white pepper

Place the scraped and washed arrowhead tubers in a two-quart saucepan, cover with water and bring quickly to a boil. Lower heat and boil for 35 minutes.

Drain in a colander and when cold, cut in quarters. Place a two-quart, thick bottomed, saucepan over high heat and melt the butter. When the foam subsides, add the flour and work the butter-flour mixture into a thick paste. Add the milk little by little until you have a thick sauce. Add the salt and pepper, and cook over low heat for 10 minutes. If the sauce is too thick, add a little more milk until desired thickness; don't make the sauce too thin. Add the quartered arrowhead tubers and reheat for at least 10 minutes. Serve with the mustard-covered porcupine meat.

SMOTHERED PORCUPINE AND ONIONS

Indian Joe remembered this recipe from his mother's day. The winter had been hard and his supply of game was long gone. There had been no meat for his family for a long time until one day he spotted a porcupine in a tall tree. Porky was soon taken care of, skinned and taken home.

As it was early in the spring, the leeks and wild onions had just poked their heads through the moss and were easily gathered.

1 porcupine	1 teaspoon spice bush powder
1 quart maple sap	1 cup cattail flour
4 tablespoons coltsfoot salt	3 tablespoons porcupine fat
1 quart cold water	5 medium wild onions
	4 leeks, white part only

The porcupine was washed and cleaned and placed in an earthenware crock. The maple sap, two tablespoons of coltsfoot salt and water were added and the crock was stored in a cold place overnight. In the morning, the porcupine was removed from the brine, disjointed and cut into serving pieces. The cattail flour, the rest of the coltsfoot salt and spice bush powder were thoroughly mixed and placed in a leather bag. The pieces of porcupine were added and the bag was thoroughly shaken to cover the meat with the flour mixture.

When the porcupine fat was sizzling in a frying pan the floured pieces were added to the pan and browned. Then the meat was removed and the finely chopped onions and leeks were added to the pan and cooked until golden brown. The meat was put back in the frying pan, more maple sap was added and the whole thing was brought to a boil, and simmered for 30 minutes. Joe recalls that never in his life had he had a meal that tasted better and, having tasted this dish, I have to agree with him.

PRAIRIE WOLF

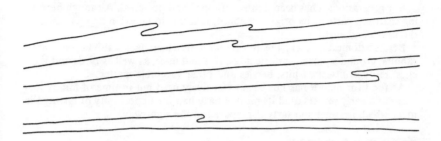

The prairie wolf, also known as the coyote or brush wolf, is a very contro-
versial animal. It ranges from Alaska through southern Canada to Quebec and
as far south as Costa Rica. The brush wolf lives a life of constant danger.

Its habit of occasionally killing livestock and wild game, and the extensive
use of its coat in the fur trade, has put a price on its head. However, being

prolific, with four to nineteen young ones every year, the prairie wolf is holding his own, thus assuring us of the thrilling experience of hearing his morning and evening serenade, so reminiscent of the Old West.

For generations it has been hunted, trapped and poisoned. Although becoming scarce in parts of its original habitat, it seems to be extending its range to the north and east.

Besides domestic stock, the prairie wolf feeds on jack rabbits, cottontail rabbits, ground squirrels, prairie dogs, rats and mice, as well as birds and their eggs, reptiles, insects, fruits, berries and other vegetable matter.

As food for man it has not been extensively used but in time of famine Indians and early settlers used its meat. I have had the opportunity of tasting the meat which is sweet and tasty if prepared in the right way.

PRAIRIE WOLF STEW

Late in the evening we arrived at Trapper Joe's cabin where a concoction was brewing on the stove. Hungry and tired, we sat down. No questions were asked until after the meal was eaten. The stew was really enjoyed — the empty pot was evidence of that. When I asked him how he had prepared the beaver, he smiled and explained that it was not beaver we had eaten but prairie wolf. He certainly fooled me.

2 pounds prairie wolf meat, or one hind leg	½ teaspoon pepper
	1 cup wild onion, chopped
3 quarts water	2 cups potatoes, diced
½ cup bacon, diced	2 cups lima beans
¼ teaspoon cayenne	2 cups fresh corn
1 teaspoon sugar	½ cup fine dry bannock
2 teaspoons salt	4 tablespoons butter

Wash and clean the prairie wolf meat. Cut into serving pieces. Place the meat in a large soup kettle, add the water, bring to a boil and then simmer for 2 hours, or until the meat is tender. Skim the surface often and discard the scum.

Remove from heat and cool. Lift the meat out of the pot, separate bones from meat and cut the meat into small pieces; returning it to the strained juices in the kettle. Add the bacon, cayenne, sugar, salt, pepper, onions, potatoes and lima beans. Put the pot back on the stove and bring to a boil. Lower heat and simmer for one hour. Add the corn and cook for 15 minutes more. Preheat the oven to 375 degrees F. Butter a three-quart fireproof casserole and add the meat stew to the casserole. Melt the butter in a small pan, add the bannock crumbs to the butter, and mix well.

Sprinkle the buttered bannock crumbs on top of the stew and bake in the oven until the crumbs are golden brown. Remove from the oven and serve directly from the casserole with red currant jelly or whole cranberries.

REINDEER

This unique animal, where both sexes carry antlers, dates back many thousands of years. Bones have been discovered with the hippopotami remains in Pleistocene formations. The Euro-Asiatic reindeer is the only domesticated species. To the Laplander, the reindeer serves as a substitute for the horse, cow, sheep and goat. It is extensively employed as a beast of burden, being used to pull sleds, or to carry men or packs on its back. The large Siberian and Kamchatkan breeds especially are used as pack animals.

A full grown animal can pull a weight of 300 pounds and travel at the rate of 100 miles a day. Its broad deeply cleft hoofs are admirably suited for travelling over broken snow.

In winter reindeer herds feed in the woods on lichens, while in summer they move to valleys to feed on herbs and shoots.

So important are these animals to the Laplanders, that they, with their entire households, accompany them on these annual migrations. In 1891 a herd of domestic reindeer was introduced to Alaska for the benefit of the natives who frequently lacked food and also as a means of transportation. The experiment proved to be so successful that it continued for ten years. At this time a sizable herd was roaming the tundra in the north.

Reindeer milk is commonly used by the Laplanders, both to feed adults and children. A very palatable reindeer cheese is often made by Laplanders, and one of the first things to be served when visiting a Lap colony is coffee with a piece of reindeer cheese in the coffee instead of cream.

I have many times feasted on reindeer meat prepared under the most primitive conditions, both in the northern part of Sweden and in the Northwest Territories, and I would like to pass on to you a few of these delicacies.

REINDEER SWISS STEAK IN PICKLE GRAVY

1½ pounds reindeer round steak
   about ¾-inch thick
1 teaspoon salt
2 tablespoons flour
½ teaspoon pepper
2 tablespoons bacon drippings
2 wild onions, sliced
2 tablespoons cattail shoots,
   finely chopped

5 cloves, whole
½ cup gherkins, thinly
   sliced
½ cup gherkin pickle juice
1 cup boiling water
2 tablespoons sugar
½ bay leaf

Trim steak free of any fat and gristle. Steak may be left whole or cut into four or five serving pieces. Wipe well with a damp cloth.

Sprinkle top with mixture of salt, flour and pepper. Pound the mixture into the steak until no whiteness remains. Turn the steak over and repeat the treatment.

Heat the bacon fat in a skillet over high heat. Add the steak and brown on both sides. Reduce heat slightly and remove meat from the skillet. Add the onions and cook until golden brown. Reduce heat to low and add the meat, cattail shoots, cloves, pickled gherkins, gherkin juice, boiling water, sugar and bay leaf. Cover the skillet and simmer for 2 hours or until meat is tender. If the meat seems dry, add more boiling water. Before serving remove bay leaf and cloves with a slotted spoon.

Serve with whole boiled potatoes and cauliflower in cheese sauce.

STUFFED REINDEER ROLLS

This recipe comes from my father's recipe book. It is delicious with smoked reindeer round roast. However, I have often used fresh reindeer meat with the same excellent results.

2 pounds smoked reindeer round
    roast, cut into ½-inch slices
6 slices bacon
1 dill pickle sliced in sixths
    lengthwise
6 anchovy fillets
2 wild onions, finely chopped

4 tablespoons flour
1 teaspoon salt
½ teaspoon pepper
4 tablespoons bacon fat
½ cup beef stock
2 tablespoons maple syrup
1 tablespoon Worcestershire
    sauce

Wipe steak clean, and remove all fat and gristle. Cut the steak into six strips, approximately two inches wide and eight inches long. Pound the steaks on both sides with a meat mallet or the edge of a plate. Place one anchovy fillet lengthwise on the meat, cover with a slice of bacon, and sprinkle the onion on top. Place one piece of the dill pickle crosswise on the bacon and roll up the meat, securing it with kitchen string or a toothpick. Combine the flour, salt and pepper and dredge the rolls in the flour mixture. Brown the rolls on all sides in the bacon fat and lower heat to a simmer. Add the beef stock, maple syrup and Worcestershire sauce, cover and simmer for 1½ hours or until the meat is tender. If the meat cooks dry, add more beef stock to keep the meat juicy and tender.

RABBIT

The rabbit is one of the most popular of the small game animals. In the New World we have a badly mixed up rabbit. In the Old World it is much easier to distinguish between the hare, which lives in a form (nest) and bears its young furred and with eyes open, and the European rabbit which lives in burrows and bears its young naked and blind.

The rabbit in the New World is hare-like in that it does not burrow and rabbit-like in that it bears its young naked and blind.

In America we have eight main species — the eastern cottontail, the brush rabbit, the pygme rabbit, the marsh rabbit, the swamp rabbit, the desert cottontail, Nuttall's cottontail, and the New England cottontail. There are also a number of sub-species. However, all rabbits have one thing in common; a delightful meal can be prepared from their white tender meat.

It is vitally important that the freshly killed animal be field dressed as soon as possible and skinned and hung for at least 8 days in a cool place to age, before any attempt is made to cook it. The meat is fine-grained and tastes very much like chicken. One thing is certain: there are as many recipes for rabbit as there are hunters and trappers.

We have carefully considered hundreds of recipes for rabbit and have included only the best ones.

BRAISED RABBIT IN WINE SAUCE

This recipe comes from Europe and I will never forget the first time I tasted it.

I was twelve years old and had participated with my father in my first large-scale rabbit hunt. After a successful day, the hunters went back to my father's hunting lodge for the night. Many tall tales were aired and my admiration for these men increased by the minute. As was the custom in camp, the hunters cooked. The first night's dinner was prepared by a grizzled old bushman, who a week before our arrival had secured the items for the menu. This is how he cooked that meal, the recipe having been pried from him many years later.

½ pound lean bacon, finely chopped	½ cup onions, finely chopped
6 pounds fresh rabbit, cut into	½ teaspoon garlic, finely chopped
serving pieces	1 cup dry red wine
½ teaspoon salt	1 cup chicken stock
½ teaspoon freshly ground	2 tablespoons brandy
pepper	1 teaspoon currant jelly
½ cup flour	1 small bay leaf

In a heavy iron pot, cook the bacon over moderate heat until crisp. Place the bacon on a juniper branch to drain. Set the pot aside.

Wash the rabbit thoroughly and pat dry. Sprinkle the pieces of meat with salt and pepper and dip them in the flour, shaking off the excess flour. Reheat the bacon fat, and when the fat splutters, add the pieces of rabbit one at a time browning them on all sides. Be careful not to burn them. Place the browned pieces on a plate and set aside. Pour off all the fat except for two tablespoons and add the onions and garlic. Stir until onions are a golden color and transparent. Add the wine and chicken stock stirring constantly. Raise heat and boil for 8 to 10 minutes. Lower and stir in the brandy and currant jelly. Add the browned rabbit meat and bay leaf. Cook over low heat for 10 minutes, then add the drained bacon and fresh lemon juice.

Cover the iron pot and simmer for 2 hours or until the meat is tender, but not falling apart.

Serve the rabbit directly from the pot with boiled whole potatoes.

RABBIT STEW WITH SOURDOUGH DUMPLINGS

This dish is also an Old World recipe and has been in my family at least since 1630, the date of the handwritten cookbook.

3 pounds fresh rabbit, cut into serving pieces	½ teaspoon salt
1 cup dry white wine	½ teaspoon black pepper
2 tablespoons white wine vinegar	¼ pound lean salt pork, diced
¼ cup olive oil	2 cups water
½ teaspoon thyme	1 tablespoon butter
1 bay leaf, crumbled	16 peeled white onions
2 teaspoons fresh parsley finely chopped	3 tablespoons shallots, chopped
	2 tablespoons flour
	2 cups beef stock
	2 tablespoons fresh dill, chopped

Wash the rabbit thoroughly and wipe dry. Combine half of the white wine, one tablespoon wine vinegar, olive oil, sliced onion, thyme, bay leaf, salt and pepper. Place in a earthenware crock and cover the rabbit with the marinade. Let stand in a cool place for 24 hours. Turn the pieces often to let the marinade penetrate all of the meat. Place the diced pork in a heavy skillet over high heat and cook until the pork is crisp and golden brown. Remove the pork with a slotted spoon and set aside. Pour off most of the fat into a mixing bowl, leaving just enough fat to cover the bottom of skillet. Add the onions and cook until golden brown, then transfer to a bowl.

Remove the rabbit from the marinade and drain. Reserve the marinade. Brown the rabbit in the skillet over high heat, adding more of the pork fat if necessary. Place the pieces of browned rabbit in a three-quart casserole. Pour off all of the fat from the skillet, add the shallots and cook, stirring constantly for 5 minutes. Stir in the flour and simmer for 2 minutes over low heat. Add the rest of the wine and beef stock. Cook over medium heat, until the sauce thickens. Pour sauce over the rabbit pieces. Preheat oven to 325 degrees F.

Bring the stew to a boil over high heat on top of the stove. Put the covered casserole in the oven and bake for 45 minutes. Remove from heat and gently stir in the onions, place the sourdough dumplings on top of the meat-onion mixture, return to the oven and cook for another 30 minutes. Just before serving, add a few teaspoons of white wine. Serve the stew directly from the casserole.

SOURDOUGH DUMPLINGS

½ cup sourdough starter	¾ teaspoon salt
1 cup milk	1 teaspoon baking powder
2½ cups unsifted flour	½ teaspoon soda
1 tablespoon sugar	

Mix the starter, milk and one cup of the flour in a large bowl. (Remember to set the starter in the morning.) Cover the bowl and keep at room temperature to rise. Turn this very soft dough out on a floured board. Combine sugar, salt, baking powder, and soda with the remaining one-half cup of flour and sift over the top of the dough.

With your hands, mix the dry ingredients into the soft dough, kneading lightly to get the right consistency. Make small balls between your floured hands, flatten them and place on top of the meat-onion mixture in the casserole.

RABBIT IN COCONUT SAUCE

While survey flying in Venezuela, one night we were treated to a special rabbit dish at the local hotel in Barinas, a small village in the foothills of the Sierra de Perija. Here, I got my first lesson in how to buy and grate coconut in a simple and effective way. When you buy a coconut, shake it to make sure that it is full of milk. To get the milk out of the nut, puncture two of the three smooth, dark eyes of the coconut by using a five inch spike or the tip of an ice pick, and with a hammer drive it through the shell. Drain out all the milk through the holes. Each coconut should yield about three-quarters of a cup of milk. Place the empty coconut in a 400 degree F. oven for about 15 minutes, then while the nut is still hot, split the shell with a hammer blow. The shell should fall away from the meat. Pare off the brown outer skin of the meat with a sharp knife or potato peeler. Cut the meat into small cubes and place them in a blender. Add the coconut milk and blend at high speed for about 2 minutes. If you don't have a blender, grate the meat through a hand grater twice and then mix with the milk.

2 cups coconut mixture
1 cup boiling water
3 medium tomatoes, seeded
  and finely chopped

1 cup onions, finely chopped
1 teaspoon salt
½ teaspoon pepper
3-4 pound rabbit, cut into
  serving pieces

Place the coconut mixture and water into a blender and purée until you have a smooth paste. If you don't have a blender, pass the mixture through a meat grinder equipped with a fine knife, several times. Using a fine sieve, press as much of the paste through as you can. (The natives did not do this and the end result was just as good). Place the purée in a flameproof casserole. Bring the casserole to a boil over high heat. Reduce heat and simmer uncovered for 15 minutes, or until the purée thickens slightly. Purée the tomatoes and onions in a large bowl, stir in the mixture in the coconut paste, season with salt and pepper. Cook for 20 minutes over low heat. Add rabbit pieces to the casserole and cover. Simmer for 1½ hours or until the meat is tender. Baste the meat with the sauce often to keep the meat moist and juicy. Serve directly from the casserole with panfried bananas.

RABBIT AND RICE CASSEROLE

While vacationing in Portugal, we often visited a local restaurant to enjoy its rabbit stew which was customarily served every Wednesday. This highly spiced dish requires a lot of dry red wine to go with it, but it is undoubtedly one of the best rabbit stews I have ever had.

½ cup dried chick-peas (garbanzos)
2 quarts water
3-pound rabbit, cut into 8
  serving pieces
1 tablespoon salt
½ teaspoon pepper
1 cup onions, finely chopped
½ cup olive oil

1 teaspoon garlic, finely
  chopped
1 small bay leaf
½ pound smoked pork sausage,
  highly seasoned
1 cup long grain rice
4 eggs, lightly beaten

Starting the day before the dish is to be served, wash the chick-peas in a sieve under cold running water. Place them in a bowl and cover with water. Soak for 12 hours at room temperature.

Drain the chick-peas and place them in a three-quart saucepan. Cover with water and bring to a boil over high heat. Reduce the heat and simmer for one hour, covered. Wash and clean the rabbit and sprinkle liberally with salt and pepper. In a skillet melt the oil over high heat. Add the rabbit and brown well, turning the pieces so that all of the meat is browned. Remove from the skillet and set aside. When the chick-peas are ready, transfer them to a four-quart flameproof casserole. Add the browned rabbit, onions, garlic, bay leaf and one-half teaspoon salt.

Mix well, cover the casserole and simmer over low heat for one hour.

Place the sausages into a small skillet and prick them with a fork in several places. Add enough water to cover completely. Bring to a boil over high heat. Reduce heat and simmer for 8 minutes uncovered. Remove sausages from the skillet and drain. Slice sausages into one-half-inch thick rounds. At the end of the cooking hour for the rabbit stew, stir in the sausages and rice. Cover and simmer for an additional 30 minutes or until the rice and rabbit mixture is tender and juicy. Most of the juices should have cooked away or been absorbed by the rice. Taste for seasoning. You might have to add more pepper as the stew should be quite peppery. Preheat the oven to 400 degrees F. Pour the beaten eggs over the contents of the casserole and bake uncovered for 10 minutes or until the eggs are set and lightly browned.

Serve as hot as possible directly from the casserole with plenty of dry red wine.

SWEET AND SOUR RABBIT

Here is a different way to prepare rabbit as introduced to us by Stella Sanders at her cottage on an island in Lake Nippissing.

2½ pound fresh rabbit
½ cup flour
½ teaspoon salt
¼ teaspoon pepper
3 tablespoons butter
1 cup maple syrup
¼ cup vinegar

½ teaspoon salt
1 cup pineapple chunks
1 medium green pepper,
  finely chopped
1½ tablespoons cornstarch
½ cup brown sugar
½ cup water

Wash the rabbit thoroughly. Pat dry and cut into eight serving pieces. Combine the flour, salt and pepper in a paper bag. Add the rabbit pieces and shake well until well coated. Melt butter in a large frying pan over high heat. When butter gives off a nutty aroma, add the rabbit pieces and brown on all sides, being careful not to burn them. Add the maple syrup, vinegar and salt. Cover the skillet and simmer over moderate heat for one hour, covered. If it cooks dry add more maple syrup. Remove from heat and add the pineapple chunks and green pepper, then cook for another 10 minutes.

In a small bowl mix the cornstarch, sugar and water. Add to the rabbit stew, stirring constantly. Let the stew simmer for 15 more minutes, then serve directly from the skillet with whole potatoes and red currant jelly.

RACCOON

This masked bandit is found all over the North American continent. He is a clever little creature who likes swampy areas where there are watercourses and adequate den sites.

The raccoon is nocturnal and is often seen wandering along stream banks in search of crayfish, frogs and other small aquatic creatures which he plucks out of the water with his long sensitive fingers. Often the food is carefully dunked and washed, piece by piece before it is eaten.

Raccoons vary greatly in size and color, but no one can mistakenly identify this rascal with his mask and his ringed tail. The raccoon's diet is varied and consists of such items as berries, corn, acorns, nuts, turtle eggs, frogs, toads, earthworms, grubs and occasionally of ground nesting birds. Sometimes he raids a chicken house or garbage can but contrary to popular opinion, the raccoon is mainly a beneficial animal.

He more than makes up for his raids on melon patches or cornfields by the great quantities of insects he consumes.

Raccoon meat is dark and red and sweet. Unfortunately the raccoon is killed for its pelt alone and the meat is not often used for food. Usually prepared in the same way as rabbit, it makes delightful eating.

If you do not like a strong gamy taste, plunge the skinned and cleaned raccoon into a pot with boiling salted water and cook for 30 minutes.

BAKED STUFFED RACCOON WITH APPLES

On a visit to trapper Jim's cabin in northern Ontario, he often served freshly killed raccoon.

1 medium raccoon	4 strips salted pork
4 large onions	2 cups beef stock

STUFFING:

5 large tart apples	1 cup dry breadcrumbs
2 tablespoons butter	1 teaspoon salt
1 teaspoon cinnamon	½ teaspoon pepper

Skin and clean the raccoon. Wash well and remove most of the fat. Place in a large soup kettle, cover with water and bring to a boil. Lower heat and simmer for 30 minutes.

Peel, core and dice the apples into a mixing bowl. Melt the butter in a small saucepan and add the cinnamon, breadcrumbs, salt and pepper. Mix well. Remove the raccoon from the cooking juices and cool. Stuff the raccoon and sew up the cavity. Place the raccoon, breast down on the rack of a roasting pan, with the legs folded under the body and fastened with kitchen string. Drape the salt pork over the back of the raccoon and fasten with toothpicks. Place the onions beside the raccoon on the rack.

Bake at 400 degrees F. for 10 minutes to brown the meat. Reduce temperature to 325 degrees and add the two cups of beef stock. Cook for one hour, basting as often as possible.

Transfer to a heated platter surrounded by the whole onions.

SKUNK

This is an animal one would not normally think of as being edible. Nevertheless its meat is sweet and very palatable.

The skunk is widely distributed throughout North America and is known to everybody, not only by its foul smell, but also by its colorful markings. It is black with two white stripes one on each side of his back. The usually bushy tail is also more or less white. Having such a formidable weapon, he seldom runs away from danger, but turns his back to his predator and fires his cannon with great accuracy.

So penetrating is the odor of his fluid that it may sometimes be perceptible a mile away, and it is so strong that clothes defiled by it can seldom be completely cleaned.

The skunk usually remains concealed during the day, but sets out in the evening at dusk to forage for worms, insects, birds, small animals and their young, and eggs of ground nesting birds. It rarely harms poultry but offsets this by eating insects, rats and mice. During the fall and winter skunk hunting is an industry of considerable importance in many regions, where he is hunted for his pelt.

After the animal is killed great care has to be taken to remove the greatly enlarged anal glands which hold the offensive fluid. These scent glands are placed one on each side of the rectum, and care should be taken not to puncture them when cleaning the carcass. When I have had skunk meat it has always been parboiled or marinated and I think either one of these methods improves it.

FRENCH FRIED SKUNK

If you want to startle your dinner guests here is a way to do it. As the meat is darker than rabbit, I usually call it wild turkey.

2 skunks, skinned and cleaned	2 egg yolks, beaten
1 tablespoon salt	3 cups milk or cream
Water to cover	1½ cups flour
2 cups vegetable oil for	½ teaspoon salt
frying	2 tablespoons baking powder

Clean and wash the skunks, making sure that the scent glands are removed. Cut up into small serving pieces. Place a soup kettle on the stove and add the meat. Cover with cold water and bring to a boil over high heat. Lower the heat and boil until meat is tender, about 35 to 40 minutes.

Remove all the scum that rises to the surface. Make a batter by mixing together the egg yolks, milk, flour, salt and baking powder. Mix thoroughly until batter has the consistency of cake batter. Heat the vegetable oil in a deep fryer at 360 degrees F. Dip the pieces of skunk in the batter, then fry them in the deep fryer until golden brown. Drain well and serve.

SKUNK SANDWICH SPREAD

A trapper friend of mine always kept either a rabbit or a skunk meat sandwich spread on hand at all times. It is excellent on an open rye sandwich.

1 cup skunk meat, cooked and ground	¼ cup cattail shoots,
2 tablespoons onion, minced	finely chopped
2 tablespoons onion, finely chopped	¼ cup sweet pickle,
2 tablespoons mint, finely chopped	finely chopped
½ cup salad dressing	

Mix all the ingredients well. Place in sealers and store in a cold place. It will keep for weeks, if not eaten long before that.

SQUIRREL

All of us have at one time or another heard the noisy chattering and scolding of the squirrel. Although the individual value of the pelt is low, it helps to supplement the trapper's and hunter's income. About fifteen genera with numerous species and sub-species are found throughout the world, except in Australia. Few native American mammals are better known or more loved than the gray squirrel. It is abundant from Canada right through to Florida and westward to Minnesota. Its food consists of nuts, acorns, seeds, fruits, etc.

Their nests or dwelling places consist of spherical structures formed of intertwined twigs with attached leaves, lined with leaves and bark.

The flesh is medium red in color, tender and has a truly delicious flavor. As this animal is so small its meat lends itself to stews and pies.

BROILED SQUIRREL

This is by far the simplest way to prepare squirrel, and it can be done either on the camp stove or on the trail.

2 squirrels	¼ teaspoon pepper
1 teaspoon salt	4 tablespoons melted bacon fat

Skin and clean the squirrels. Wash and pat dry. Cut in half lengthwise and remove the head. Rub the squirrels with salt and pepper. If in camp, place the halved squirrels on a broiling rack and brush with the bacon fat. Broil eight inches away from heat for 30 minutes. Baste every 5 minutes with bacon fat.

If on the trail, spear the whole squirrel on a stick and put it in front of the camp fire, basting and turning the stick occasionally for at least 45 minutes. A few apples on a stick propped in front of the fire will complement this dish very well.

SQUIRREL AND MUSHROOM CASSEROLE

Often the easiest way to prepare squirrel meat in the hunt camp is to make a casserole the night before. Trapper Jim often did this and here is one of his specialities.

2 squirrels, cleaned and cut into serving pieces	½ tablespoon mint, finely chopped
2 teaspoons salt	1 teaspoon salt
Water	¼ teaspoon pepper
3 tablespoons flour	1 cup mushrooms

Place the squirrel meat into a large soup kettle. Cover with water and add two teaspoons salt. Bring to a boil over high heat, lower heat and simmer for 1½ hours. Remove and discard the scum as it rises to the surface. Take the squirrels out of the kettle and cool to room temperature. Using a sharp knife, cut the meat from the bones and cube it. Strain the broth and pour into a three-quart saucepan. Add the flour, mint, salt, pepper, mushrooms to the broth stirring constantly. Cook for 20 minutes. Add the meat and cook for another 10 minutes. Pour into a well-greased casserole. If you like, cover the meat with a layer of biscuit dough.

BISCUIT MIX:

2 cups flour	¼ cup bacon fat
4 teaspoons baking powder	¾ cup milk
1 teaspoon salt	

Sift together the flour, baking powder and salt. Cut in the fat and add the milk. Stir until all the ingredients are moistened. Roll out and cut into rounds. Preheat the oven to 400 degrees F. Put the biscuits on top of the stew in the casserole. Bake until biscuits are golden brown, about 15 minutes.

SQUIRREL ROYALE SOUP

Tom Adams, a former trapper, lumber camp cook, and chef has often served this soup at our hunt camp on our annual hunting trips.

3 hard-cooked egg yolks	4 tablespoons butter
2 cups squirrel meat, cooked	4 tablespoons flour
1 cup stale bread crumbs	1 quart squirrel stock
1 pint milk	1 teaspoon salt
	½ teaspoon pepper

Rub the egg yolks and squirrel meat through a sieve. Put in a mixing bowl and add the bread crumbs. Stir in one-half cup of milk and soak well. Heat the butter in a three-quart saucepan, blend in the flour and add the boiling squirrel stock, a little at a time. Add the remaining milk, scalded. Simmer for 5 minutes. Add the squirrel mixture gradually and season to taste. Cook for 5 minutes over low heat. Do not let the soup come to a boil. Serve as hot as possible.

CREAM SOUP WITH SQUIRREL MEAT

This is another one of Tom's special soup dishes.

1 pound butter	8 raw arrowhead tubers,
4 wild leeks, cleaned and	peeled and sliced
minced	12 cups squirrel stock
4 wild onions, minced	2 cups squirrel meat, minced
1 cup sheep sorrel, cleaned	4 cups cream
and minced	4 teaspoons chives, chopped

Melt the butter in a three-quart saucepan, add the wild leeks and onions and cook for 4 minutes. Add the sheep sorrel, arrowhead tubers, squirrel stock and minced squirrel meat. Season to taste. Bring to a boil, lower heat and cook for 30 minutes. Rub the mixture through a fine sieve into a large bowl. Place the bowl on ice or in the snow to cool. When really cold, beat in the cream and taste for seasoning. Sprinkle the chopped chives on top of the dish and serve, well mixed and cold.

SQUIRREL PIE

Once while hunting rabbits, we were lucky enough to get several medium-sized squirrels as well. The camp cook made squirrel pies, and here is the way he did it.

3 squirrels, skinned and cleaned,
  cut into serving pieces
Water
2 teaspoons salt
½ teaspoon pepper
2 bay leaves
1 carrot, finely chopped
3 wild onions, finely chopped
3 stalks cattail shoots, diced

1 cup butter
1 cup flour
3 cups squirrel stock
1 cup cream
1 cup salt pork, cooked and cubed
6 wild onions, whole
6 boiled potatoes, diced
2 teaspoons Worcestershire sauce
Pie paste

Put the squirrel pieces into a large enamel pot, add water to cover and one teaspoon salt. Let stand overnight in a cool place. Transfer to a large soup kettle, cover with water and let come to a fast boil. Lower heat and cook for 5 minutes. Drain off the water.

Cover with clean hot water and add the rest of the salt, pepper, bay leaves, carrots, wild onions and cattail stalks. Bring to a boil, lower heat and simmer for one hour or until squirrel meat is tender.

Transfer the squirrels to a large platter; strain the squirrel stock and save.

Melt the butter in a three-quart saucepan, add the flour and stir. Add the squirrel stock a little at a time and blend in the cream. Cook for half an hour over low heat. Add the salt pork, boiled onions, boiled potatoes and Worcestershire sauce. Cook for 10 minutes or until the onions and potatoes are heated through. Place the squirrel meat in a three-quart fireproof casserole and pour the velouté sauce over the meat. Cover the casserole with pie paste and bake for 20 minutes in a moderate oven (325 degrees F.)

MOTHER'S PIE CRUST

No one can make pie crust like Mother does. So here is the recipe for the world's best pie crust.

½ cup boiling water
1 cup soft lard (Not shortening)
1 teaspoon salt

3 cups all purpose flour
¼ teaspoon baking powder

Pour the boiling water into a bowl and add the lard. The lard should be quite soft but not melted. Mix well, using a fork, until all lard is melted and mixture is like thick cream. If the lard is too hard to melt in the water, place the bowl over hot water until the lard has melted.

Add the flour, salt and baking powder. Mix well using fingers to finish mixing. Make a ball of the dough and place in a bowl. Refrigerate overnight.

Remove from refrigerator 2 hours before you want to use it. This recipe will make two large two-crust pies. Wrap what is left over in Saran wrap and freeze. It can be kept for months.

Chapter 15

GAME BIRDS

Game birds are plentiful on this continent. Bird hunting is a popular sport today, not only because it is challenging, but also because most birds properly prepared, are delicious.

What is better than an early stroll in the bush on a frosty fall morning with all senses alert in the hopes of outwitting the birds!

Unfortunately, too many birds are spoiled because of improper care in the field. I am sure that there are just as many methods of field dressing game birds in the bush as there are bird hunters.

It really doesn't matter which method you use as long as the bird is taken care of immediately after it has been killed. Many bird-hunters maintain that birds can be carried all day without cleaning, but if the weather is warm and the birds are to be kept more than one day, chances of spoilage increase. It is well worth cleaning the bird at once. I have hunted with many professional hunters and trappers and they all agree that birds should be cleaned as soon as possible.

I field-dress my birds by plucking a strip of feathers from the breastbone to the vent and with a sharp knife I make a shallow cut along this line, encircling the vent, making sure that I cut only through the skin and the thin layer of meat without puncturing the intestines. Then I insert two or three fingers through this opening and reach as far up to the neck as possible, rotating my hand to loosen all the organs and to bring the viscera out intact. I then wash the cavity with cold water to remove all blood and stuff it with fresh cut evergreen boughs.

A bird should hang to age for about six days in a cold place before any attempt is made to cook it. This aging is most important to get the meat tender and tasty.

DUCK ON THE TRAIL

1 duck	½ cup flour
1 teaspoon salt	½ cup bacon fat
½ teaspoon pepper	1 cup milk

Pluck and clean the duck. Wash well in cold water. Cut duck into eight pieces. Rub the salt and pepper into the meat and roll in the flour. Place the frying pan on the campfire, add the bacon fat and heat over high heat. Place the floured pieces of duck in the frying pan and fry until brown on all sides. Simmer in the fat for about 30 minutes. Add the milk, cover the pan tightly and simmer over low heat for one hour or until the meat is tender and juicy. Serve with fresh bannock.

JELLIED GOOSE

This recipe comes from an old homestead in Saskatchewan and was taken from a handwritten recipe book which had been in the family for many years.

1 6 to 8-pound goose	3 egg whites and the crushed
1 quart water	shells of the eggs
1 teaspoon salt	2 envelopes gelatin
½ pound pork shank	¼ cup water
5 white peppercorns	2 apples peeled and sectioned
3 bay leaves	10 cooked prunes
¾ cup vinegar	

Place the plucked and cleaned goose in a large soup kettle. Add the water, salt and pork shank. Bring to a boil over high heat, then lower heat and simmer for 2 hours. Do this the day before the meat is going to be used. Cool meat in the juices as quickly as possible. The next day remove the goose from the cooking juices, place on a platter and skim off the fat from the stock. Bring the stock to a boil again and add the peppercorns, bay leaves and vinegar. Cook with the spices 15 to 20 minutes. Clarify with the egg whites and crushed egg shells. Remove from heat, strain the juices through a fine sieve and measure the quantity.

For each quart of stock, use two envelopes of gelatin. Sprinkle the gelatin over one-quarter cup of water, then add the boiling stock. Remove from heat and pour a little in bottom of a wet mold and let set.

Cut the meat into slices and place decoratively in the mold. Pour the jelly over the meat and place in a cool place to set. To serve the following day, unmold on a platter and garnish with sections of cooked apples and cooked prunes.

BREAST OF PARTRIDGE

"The Hunt Camp Special", I like to call this dish, because it is fast and easy to prepare and is usually a hit with hungry and tired hunters. Here is the recipe.

4 portions partridge breast	½ teaspoon pepper
8 slices bacon	4 slices toast
1 teaspoon salt	1 can cream of mushroom soup

Cut four portions of breast from a good-sized partridge. Roll each breast in two slices of bacon and fasten with tooth picks. Season with salt and pepper and place under the broiler for 15 minutes. Toast four pieces of white bread. Heat the cream of mushroom soup in a small saucepan. Place the toast on a platter and put one piece of partridge breast on each piece of toast. Pour the cream of mushroom soup over the meat and the toast and sprinkle with finely chopped watercress.

PARTRIDGE IN BURGUNDY

My hunting companion and trapper, Carl Haintz's great-grandfather and his wife brought this delightful dish with them from the Old World. I have had similar dishes but none can compete with Carl's way of preparing this gourmet dinner.

4 one-pound, oven ready young partridges	2 tablespoons salt pork, chopped and cooked
1 teaspoon salt	2 cups Burgundy wine
½ teaspoon pepper	3 tablespoons brandy
1 cup flour	¼ teaspoon dried thyme
10 tablespoons butter	¼ teaspoon dried tarragon
¼ cup onion, finely chopped	1 bay leaf
2 cups thinly sliced mushrooms (chantrelle if possible)	¼ teaspoon ground nutmeg
	2 tablespoons dill, finely chopped

Clean and wash the birds under running water. Pat dry inside and out. Rub the birds with salt and pepper, then roll them in the flour, shaking off excess flour. In a heavy frying pan, melt five tablespoons of butter over moderate heat. Brown the birds on all sides until golden.

Remove the birds from the frying pan and set aside on a platter. Add two more tablespoons of butter to the frying pan and add the onions. Cook over moderate heat until the onions are golden, drop in the mushrooms and the salt pork. Cook for ten minutes stirring constantly. Transfer the onion-mushroom mixture to a bowl and set aside.

Melt the rest of the butter on high heat, then add the rest of the onions. Cook for two or three minutes, until the onions are soft and lightly colored. Add the wine and brandy, and bring to a boil, scraping the bottom and sides of the frying pan. Add the thyme, tarragon, bay leaf and nutmeg. Season to taste with salt and pepper. Return the birds to the frying pan and baste well. Reduce the heat to low, cover the pan and simmer for thirty-five minutes, or until the birds are tender. Remove the birds from the pan and place on a heated platter. Cover with foil and let rest.

Bring the cooking juices in the frying pan to a boil and boil briskly until the liquid is reduced to about one cup.

Remove the bay leaf with a slotted spoon, then stir in the onion-mushroom-salt pork mixture and simmer for 5 minutes or until the mixture is thoroughly heated. Stir in the chopped dill. Serve sauce separately. I like boiled potatoes and cranberry sauce to accompany this dish.

ROAST STUFFED DUCK

2 ducks, oven ready	2 oranges, peeled and quartered
2 tablespoons red wine	10 prunes, soaked in water
Salt	4 tablespoons butter
Pepper	2 squares heavy foil

Wash the ducks in cold running water. Place the ducks in a stainless steel pot, cover with cold water and add the red wine. Let stand for 2 hours. Remove the birds from the pot, pat them dry and rub inside and out with salt and pepper.

Stuff the ducks loosely with the oranges and the prunes. Lace the openings with a skewer and string. Place the ducks in the middle of the heavy foil. Smear with the butter and enclose in the foil. Preheat the oven to 375 degrees F. Place the ducks individually wrapped on the rack of a roasting pan. Cook for one hour. Remove from the oven, fold back the foil from the breasts of the ducks and broil for 6 minutes or until the ducks are golden brown.

GROUSE SOUP

Trapper Joe usually had a few birds hanging and I very seldom visited his cabin when a soup kettle was not brewing on the stove. This recipe was one of his favorites.

2 large grouse, cleaned and cut into serving pieces	½ pound moose meat cut in strips, or stewing meat
½ pound salt pork, cubed	3 quarts water
4 wild onions, finely chopped	1 cup cattail shoots, cut into one-inch lengths
1 teaspoon salt	
½ teaspoon pepper	2 tablespoons butter
2 tablespoons butter	4 pieces fried white bread

Wash the grouse under running cold water. Pat dry and cut in small serving pieces. Place in a large soup kettle. Melt the butter in a heavy skillet over high heat. When the butter gives off a nutty aroma, lower heat and add the cubed salt pork and onions. Cook until onions are golden brown. Add the onion-pork mixture to the soup kettle. Place the strips of moose meat on top. Add the salt, pepper and the three quarts of cold water. Bring to a boil over high heat, lower heat and simmer gently for 2 hours, removing as it rises to the surface. Transfer bird pieces to a heated platter, cover lightly with a piece of foil and set aside. Let the soup cook for another hour.

Remove from heat, strain through a fine sieve into a large saucepan, add the cattail stalks and simmer for 15 minutes.

Place the skillet back on the fire and add two tablespoons of butter. When the butter is sizzling, add the four pieces of white bread and fry until golden brown on both sides.

Cut each slice of bread into four pieces and add to soup tureen. Transfer bird pieces to the tureen and pour soup over the bread and birds. Cut the moose meat into serving pieces and serve as a side dish, with the soup.

ROAST GOOSE WITH FIDDLEHEAD STUFFING

This dish is a favorite of mine, because it brings out the true flavor of goose.

4 pounds fiddleheads	2 cups crabapples,
1 orange	finely chopped
1 cup arrowhead tubers, grated	1 tablespoon caraway seeds
6 tablespoons butter	1 8-10 pound goose
3 cups wild onions, chopped	Salt and pepper

Preheat the oven to 350 degrees F. Remove the brown coating on the fiddle-heads by rubbing them between your hands, then wash under cold running water.

Peel the orange and squeeze juice into a large mixing bowl, removing all seeds. Peel the arrowhead tubers and grate very finely to make one cup. Add to the orange juice and stir well, making sure that the grated tubers are thoroughly coated with juice.

Heat the butter over high heat in a twelve-inch skillet until it gives off a nutty aroma. Reduce heat and add the onions. Cook until onions are golden brown. Add the fiddleheads, apples and caraway seeds. Simmer for 10 minutes stirring occasionally. Transfer mixture to the mixing bowl containing the tubers and orange.

Wash the goose inside and out, and pat dry. Sprinkle the cavity generously with salt and pepper. Fill the goose with the fiddlehead stuffing, sew up the openings and truss the legs with cord. Set the goose, breast side up, on a rack in a large roasting pan. Cook in the middle of the oven for 2½ hours or 25 minutes per pound. With a bulb baster, remove all the fat that drips into the pan. The goose is ready when the juices from a punctured thigh run pale yellow.

Remove to a serving platter and cut away the thread and cord. Transfer the stuffing to a serving dish. Let the goose rest for at least 20 minutes before carving it.

WILD DUCK À LA BERGLUND

I have used this recipe on many occasions and found it particularly satisfactory if a less gamier taste is desired.

2 large ducks, cleaned and
   oven-ready
Salt
Pepper
2 large apples, peeled,
   cored and chopped

¾ cup cattail
   shoots, chopped
¼ cup mint, chopped
1 cup apple juice
3 tablespoons butter
¼ cup brandy

Wash the ducks inside and out. Pat dry. Rub with salt and pepper, inside and out. Mix together in a large mixing bowl the apples, cattail shoots and mint. Use half of the mixture to stuff the birds. Lace and truss, then sprinkle with salt. Arrange the birds breast side up on a rack in a shallow roasting pan and with a fork prick the breasts. Preheat oven to 325 degrees F.

Roast for one hour. Pour off the fat and add the apple juice, butter and brandy. Continue roasting and basting frequently with pan juices until tender. Remove the birds to a platter and keep warm. Skim fat from the pan drippings and add enough apple juice to make two cups. Stir in two tablespoons of flour mixed with an equal amount of skimmed fat. Cook and stir until thickened and smooth. Adjust seasonings.

BRAISED PHEASANT WITH PLANTAIN

This recipe comes from our book *The Edible Wild* and many people who have tried it have liked it.

2 pheasants
1 tablespoon salt
½ pound butter, softened
1 pound plantain leaves
2 tablespoons butter

¼ cup vegetable oil
½ cup water
1 cup heavy cream
¼ cup white wine

Pluck and draw the pheasants. Wash thoroughly inside and out. Pat dry with paper towels. Rub salt over inside and outside of birds. Using an electric beater set at medium, cream the butter. With your hands, spread half of the butter inside each bird.

Clean and wash the plantain leaves and discard bruised or darkened leaves. Stuff the birds with the leaves, making sure the cavities are well filled. Sew them up and tie the legs together so that they will hold their shape while cooking.

Preheat the oven to 350 degrees F. In a twelve-inch skillet heat two tablespoons of butter over high heat. When it gives off a nutty aroma, moderate the heat and add the oil. Stir well. Put the pheasants, one at a time, breast side down in the skillet. After about 7 minutes, turn the birds and cook for 7 minutes more. Continue turning until both birds are browned on all sides.

Transfer the pheasants to a roasting pan big enough to hold both birds easily. Pour the water into the skillet and bring to a boil, stirring to get all the browned bits off the bottom. Pour the contents of the skillet over the birds, which have been placed in the roasting pan breast up. Cover tightly and braise in the middle of the oven for 1½ hours.

Remove the pheasants to a carving board and let rest for 5 minutes, Skim and discard the fat from the pan juices. Add the cream and bring to a boil, stirring constantly and scraping any browned bits off the bottom of the pan. Boil the sauce briskly for several minutes and add the wine.

Let the cream and the wine reduce and the sauce thicken. Season to taste and serve in a gravy boat.

FRICASSEÉ DE PERDREAUX À L'ANCIENNE
(Old Fashioned Partridge Fricassee)

Once when bird hunting in Quebec I was served this delightful dish. As all colonial cooking means a day's work, a long time goes into the preparation of all these old recipes. In this case, all the work is well worthwhile.

3 partridges, cleaned and oven
   ready, cut into serving pieces
8 tablespoons butter
Salt
White pepper
¼ cup flour
3 cups partridge stock
Bouquet garni, made of 4
parsley sprigs and 1 bay leaf,
tied together

½ teaspoon dried thyme
¾ cup chicken stock
24 wild onions, peeled
¾ cup fresh mushrooms, whole
1 teaspoon vinegar
2 egg yolks
½ cup heavy cream
2 tablespoons fresh parsley,
   finely chopped

Wash the partridges thoroughly in cold water. Dry with a damp cloth. In a heavy three-quart heatproof casserole, melt six tablespoons butter over moderate heat. Fry a few pieces of partridge at a time, turning until no longer pink. Remove to a platter and season with salt and pepper.

Stir the flour into the remaining butter in the casserole and cook over low heat stirring constantly for 2 minutes. Remove from heat. Slowly pour in the partridge stock, beating vigorously to blend roux and liquid. Return to heat and, while stirring constantly, let the sauce thicken and come to a boil. Reduce heat and simmer for 2 minutes.

Return the partridges to the casserole together with the juices that have collected on the plate. Add the bouquet garni and thyme. The sauce should cover the partridges. Bring to a boil, reduce heat and simmer for 45 minutes.

Put chicken into a ten-inch skillet over medium heat. Add two tablespoons of butter and the onions. Bring to a boil, cover and simmer for 15 minutes or until the onions are tender when pierced. Using a slotted spoon, transfer the onions to a bowl and set aside. Add the vinegar and mushrooms to the remaining stock. Bring to a boil and simmer for 10 minutes. Remove the mushrooms and place them with the onions in the bowl. Boil the remaining liquid until reduced to two tablespoons, and pour it over the partridges.

Remove the partridges from the casserole and transfer them to a plate. Discard the bouquet garni. Skim the fat from the surface of the sauce. Blend the egg yolks and cream and whisk into the hot sauce, a few tablespoons at a time, until about half a cup has been added. Bring to a boil, stirring constantly. Boil slowly for one minute. Taste for seasoning. Strain through a fine sieve into a large bowl.

Clean the casserole, arrange the partridge pieces, onions, and mushrooms in it, and pour the sauce over them. Before serving, cover the casserole and simmer it over moderate heat for 10 minutes, or until the partridges are hot. Do not let the sauce come to a boil again. Serve directly from the casserole which at the last minute has been sprinkled with chopped fresh parsley.

Chapter 16

FISH

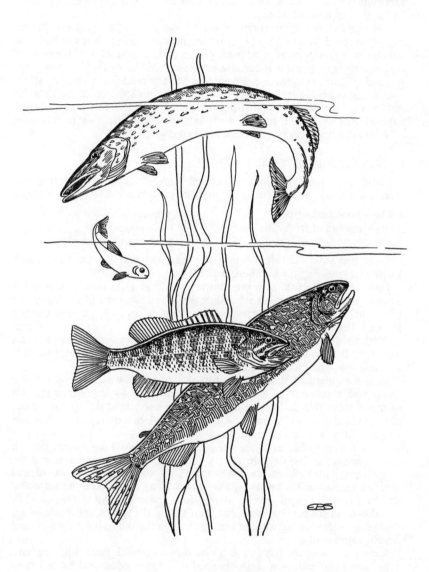

From Canada's northern icy coastal waters, to Florida's balmy Gulf Stream we have an abundance of fish. Fish has always been important to the diet of people in North America. Fish used to be a great staple food of the Indians as well as the early settlers.

Fish is an excellent source of protein, and is easily digested by people of all ages. But fish can easily be over-cooked or dried out in the oven until it tastes like a piece of decayed wood.

You could serve a different type of fish for every day of the year without repeating yourself. What a bounty nature has bestowed on us! It is too bad that man has polluted so many good fishing lakes and streams. One of the reasons why fishing is so popular is because equipment can be as simple or as complicated as you care to make it. I have seen Indians catch just as many fish on a simple bone hook as the affluent fisherman with his $500 outfit. As a matter of fact, the bent pin-hook and string has pulled out more fish than the most sophisticated equipment. In an earlier chapter we discussed how to take care of your catch and how to prepare it for cooking.

MARINATED LAKE TROUT IN DILL

I have in my possession a three hundred year-old recipe for preparing and storing fresh fish, and here it is. Salmon may be substituted for lake trout.

1 4 to 5 pound lake trout	**½ cup sugar**
2 large bunches of fresh dill	**2 tablespoons white**
½ cup coarse salt	**peppercorns, crushed**

Clean and scale the fish. Remove the head and tail. Cut the fish in half lengthwise removing the backbone and the small bones as well.

Place half of the fish, skin side down, in a large glass casserole. (I use a wooden box big enough to accommodate the largest fish I intend to pickle. The box is lined with plastic to prevent leakage of juices and when in use the plastic is lined with aluminum foil.)

Wash the dill and shake dry. Chop the dill into small pieces and sprinkle on top of the fish. In a bowl, combine the salt, sugar and crushed peppercorns. Sprinkle this mixture over the fish.

Place the other half of the fish on top of the herbs and spices, skin side up. Cover with aluminum foil and set a heavy platter slightly larger than the fish on top of them. Weigh down with three or four heavy food tins. (I cut a piece of board so that it just fits inside the box, then I place it on top of the fish and weigh it down with five or six bricks.)

Store in a cool place or in the refrigerator for at least 3 days. Turn the fish every 6 hours the first day, then every 12 hours, replacing the cover and the weights every time. When the fish is ready, transfer to a cutting board and separate the halves. With a table knife, scrape away the dill and the seasoning and pat dry with a paper towel or damp cloth. Place one half of the fish, skin side down, on the carving board and start slicing the fish halves thinly on an angle diagonal to the tail without cutting through the skin. This is a traditional Swedish supper dish.

Keep the rest of the fish in a large earthenware crock filled with the salt-sugar brine marinade and fresh chopped dill. Often additional brine has to be made by boiling one gallon of water and adding enough salt to make the brine strong enough to float an egg. Add a few bunches of finely chopped dill and cool. Fish prepared in this way keeps for a year.

FISH BALLS

This recipe comes from the same source as the previous one and is about three hundred years old. The only changes we have made are to take out the back breaking labor by using modern equipment.

1½ pounds of any white fish cleaned and boned, and cut into small pieces	1 cup heavy cream
½ cup light cream	2 teaspoons salt
	1 teaspoon white pepper
	1½ tablespoons cornstarch

Place fish pieces, a few at a time, in an electric blender. In a bowl, mix the light and heavy cream. Add a few spoonfuls of the mixed cream to the blender bowl. Blend at high speed, turning the machine off after a few minutes to scrape down the purée from the sides of the jar.

Continue to blend, one batch at a time, until you have a smooth purée and the fish is used up, using as much of the cream as is necessary to form a smooth purée.

Place the purée in a large mixing bowl. Beat in the salt, pepper and 1½ tablespoons of cornstarch. Slowly add any left over cream and beat vigorously until the mixture is very light and fluffy. Place the bowl in the refrigerator or in a cool place for at least one hour, then roll about one tablespoon of the fish mixture in your hands to make one-inch balls. Place a two to three-quart saucepan on the stove. Add water, bring to a boil and add one teaspoon salt. Lower heat to a slow simmer. Drop the balls in the water and boil for 5 minutes, or until firm to the touch. Place balls in sterilized jars. Strain the cooking juices and fill the jars with them. Seal and store in a cool place. To use, make a shrimp sauce and empty one jar of fish balls into the sauce. Heat and serve with boiled potatoes.

SHRIMP SAUCE

4 tablespoons butter	1½ pounds medium shrimps, cooked and finely chopped, or 2 cans medium shrimps
4 tablespoons flour	
2 cups milk	
½ cup heavy cream	1 cup juice from the cooked shrimps or the juice from the canned shrimps
1 teaspoon pepper	

In a two-quart stainless steel saucepan, melt the butter over high heat. Lower heat and stir in the flour. Mix until small balls have formed. Remove from heat and add the milk and cream all at once. Add the pepper, stirring constantly with a wire whisk. Keep heat low and simmer until the sauce is smooth and creamy. Add the juice and blend well. Cook for another 5 minutes, then add the finely chopped shrimps and heat thoroughly before adding the fish balls.

BOILED SMELTS IN DILL

This is also an age-old recipe.

1 pound fresh smelts	1 bunch of dill, finely chopped
1 quart water	½ cup vinegar
1 teaspoon salt	2 tablespoons sugar
½ teaspoon white pepper	

Remove the heads and innards of the fish. Using your thumb, split the fish and remove the backbone. Roll the filleted fish skin side out, and place in a flameproof casserole. Combine the water, salt, pepper, dill, vinegar and sugar and mix well, then add the mixture to the casserole until it covers the fish. Reserve the rest.

Place the casserole on top of the stove and bring to a boil. Lower heat and add more of the vinegar mixture. Simmer for 10 minutes. Remove from heat and cool to room temperature, then place in the refrigerator to jelly. Serve chilled.

BAKED PICKEREL STUFFED WITH WATERCRESS

This is a delightful way to prepare any large fresh-water fish, such as pickerel, pike or lake trout.

1 3-pound pickerel	½ cup parsley, finely chopped
1 cup wild rice	¼ cup leeks, finely chopped
2 cups watercress	1 tablespoon salt
½ cup wild onions, minced	3 tablespoons heavy cream
2 tablespoons butter	8 tablespoons soft butter
2 hard-boiled eggs, chopped	½ cup dry white wine

Clean the pickerel under cold running water. Dry with a damp cloth. Remove the backbone, but leave the head and tail on. Set aside.

In a heavy three-quart saucepan, bring two quarts of water to a boil. Add one-quarter of a teaspoon salt and pour in the wild rice in a slow stream so that the water does not stop boiling. Simmer for 20 minutes or until the rice is still slightly firm. Drain in a large sieve and place the sieve over the saucepan to dry.

In a small bowl, toss the watercress with the onion. Melt the butter over high heat. When it gives off a nutty aroma, lower the heat and add the watercress-onion mixture. Cook for 5 minutes, then transfer to a large mixing bowl and add the chopped eggs, cooked rice, parsley and leeks. Season to taste and add the heavy cream. Mix thoroughly.

Stuff the fish with this filling and sew up the opening.

Preheat the oven to 375 degrees F. In a baking dish, melt eight tablespoons of butter over moderate heat. Place the fish on its side in the dish, raise the heat and cook the fish until it is golden brown (about 10 minutes). Turn the fish over and brown on the other side.

Remove the fish, being careful not to break it apart and drain the butter into a small bowl. Line the baking dish with a piece of aluminum foil and, using a pastry brush, add the reserved butter and grease the foil. Tie a string from the snout of the fish around the tail so it will stand upright in a nice curve, and set it on the foil. Pour the wine into the bottom of the baking dish and place in the oven. Lower the heat to 350 degrees F. and bake for 20 minutes, basting with a bulb baster every 5 minutes. When the fish is almost cooked, raise the heat for 5 minutes and bake until golden brown.

Remove from the oven and carefully slide the fish from the foil onto a heated platter. Remove the string and serve at once with melted butter in a separate dish.

GRILLED MARINATED CATFISH

Homer Blais, an old woodsman friend once served me this dish. I have eaten catfish prepared in many ways, but I think this is the best.

2 tablespoons olive oil	2 teaspoons onions, finely
1 tablespoon vinegar	chopped
½ teaspoon salt	2 catfish, 1-pound each
¼ teaspoon pepper	3 tablespoons combined butter
	and vegetable oil

Remove the slime from the fish with paper towels. Remove the head and backbone without cutting them in half. Preheat the broiler. Use a shallow baking dish large enough to hold the fish flat in a single layer. Mix in a small bowl the oil, vinegar, salt, pepper and onions and pour over the fish in the baking dish. The fish should have been placed with the skin side down. Let it sit this way for 20 minutes, then turn the fish over and soak in the marinade for another 20 minutes. Brush the broiler rack with the oil-butter mixture, and place the catfish, skin side down on the rack about three inches from the source of heat for 15 minutes. Grill only on one side, basting from time to time with the melted oil-butter mixture. After the fish has turned golden brown and flaky, serve at once with horseradish butter.

HORSERADISH BUTTER

8 tablespoons butter	¼ teaspoon salt
2 tablespoons freshly grated	¼ teaspoon dry mustard
horseradish root or two	¼ teaspoon white pepper
tablespoons bottled horse radish	

Cream the butter with a spoon or with an electric beater until it is light and fluffy. Mix in the grated horseradish (if you are using bottled horse-radish, drain well to remove all the fluid) salt, dry mustard and pepper. Beat in the dry ingredients. Mix well until smooth and thick.

Transfer horseradish butter to a small serving dish and keep in refrigerator until you are ready to serve. Serve cold, in squares on top of the grilled catfish fillets.

PAN FRIED TROUT IN SOUR CREAM

While on a fishing trip in the northern part of Sweden with a Laplander as guide, our cream had gone sour, but our fishing luck was great and this is the way he prepared our meal

4 fresh trout about ½ pound each,	½ cup flour
cleaned but with head and tail	6 tablespoons butter
left on	1 cup sour cream
Salt	½ teaspoon vinegar

Wash the trout in cold water. Pat dry inside and out with a cloth. Rub salt into the cavities of the fish, roll in the flour and shake off any excess.

In a heavy iron frying pan, melt four tablespoons of butter over high heat. When the butter gives off a nutty aroma, lower heat and fry the trout two at a time for about 8 minutes on each side, turning the fish carefully so that they won't break. Transfer to a platter which can be kept warm. Cover with aluminum foil if you have any, or if at home, place in a 200 degree F. oven.

Add the two tablespoons of butter, stir over low heat scraping up the brown pan drippings with a wooden spoon. Add the sour cream a little at a time stirring constantly. Cook for about 5 minutes without letting the cream boil. Stir in the vinegar. Simmer for 5 more minutes and pour the sauce over the fish.

DILL-JELLIED EEL

This is a wonderful way to prepare this fish and was often used in the old days.

3 pounds eel	10 whole peppercorns
2 tablespoons coarse salt	2 teaspoons salt
2½ cups water	2 bay leaves
¼ cup white wine	¼ cup fresh lemon juice
2 wild onions, finely chopped	2 tablespoons fresh dill
2 bunches fresh dill	

Skin the eel. An easy way to do this is to make a shallow cut around the neck behind the fins. Wrap the head in a piece of newspaper, grab the skin with a pair of pliers and pull towards the tail. Then slit the eel open and remove the entrails.

Cut the eel into two-inch pieces and wash well under running water. Place in a single layer in a shallow pan. Sprinkle with coarse salt and pour in enough boiling water to cover the pieces completely. Soak for 10 minutes, drain and rinse thoroughly under running cold water.

Place the eel in a fireproof casserole. Add the water, wine, onion, dill, peppercorns, salt and bay leaves. Bring to a boil over high heat. Reduce heat and simmer for 20 minutes. Remove from heat, stir in the vinegar and sprinkle the finely chopped dill on top.

When thoroughly chilled, the liquid should form a soft jelly. Serve from the casserole.

SMELTS IN MARINADE

In the spring when smelts are in abundance it is convenient to be able to prepare this fish in many different ways. Here is another way.

1 cup white vinegar	1 cup flour
1 cup water	2 teaspoons salt
½ cup sugar	1 teaspoon pepper
20 smelts, cleaned	6 tablespoons butter

Wash the cleaned smelts under cold running water. Remove heads and tails with a sharp knife. In a large mixing bowl, mix the vinegar, water and sugar. Mix well and place in the refrigerator. The marinade should be made at least one hour before it is to be used.

In a small paper bag, mix one cup of flour, two teaspoons salt and one teaspoon pepper. Close the bag and shake well to mix. Drop in five or six smelts at a time. Close the bag and shake well. Put the floured smelts on a plate, removing the excess flour.

Heat the butter in a twelve-inch skillet over high heat until the butter gives off a nutty aroma. Add as many of the smelts as the pan will hold without crowding them.

Cook for 5 minutes turning the fish once, until the fish are golden brown on all sides. Remove to a double thickness of paper towels and drain. Before fish cool, put them in the marinade and refrigerate.

Serve well chilled.

DILL-FLAVORED CRAYFISH

This little fresh water crustacean is often overlooked as food on this continent, but anyone who has participated in a crayfish party in one of the Scandinavian countries will appreciate this dish.

3 quarts cold water	**30 live fresh-water crayfish**
½ cup salt	*garnish:*
3 bunches of fresh dill	**1 bunch of fresh dill**

In a large enameled soup-kettle, combine the water, salt and three bunches of dill tied together. Bring to a boil over high heat and boil briskly, uncovered for 15 minutes. Wash the crayfish carefully under running cold water. Then drop them a few at a time, into the boiling water. Wait until the water is at a rolling boil again, then add a few more.

When all of the crayfish are in the kettle, cover tightly and boil for about 10 minutes. Line a large bowl with the last of the bunches of dill, using only the crowns. Remove the kettle from the heat, and with a slotted spoon, transfer the crayfish from the kettle to the bowl, placing them on top of the dill.

Strain the stock through a fine sieve over the crayfish, and let them rest in the juice in a cold place until they reach room temperature. Cover the bowl and refrigerate for at least 12 hours. About 3 hours before the crayfish are to be served, take the bowl out of the refrigerator and let the crayfish come to room temperature. Drain and pile them high on a platter. Garnish with sprigs of fresh dill.

Chapter 17
CAKES AND DESSERTS

There was nothing so rewarding to a pioneer wife as to be able to put on the table a good cake or dessert after a hearty meal. The cake or the dessert had two functions. Firstly, it was often served on the day of rest to make it more sabbath-like and as a marker in an otherwise gray, every-day diet. Secondly, it gave the housewife a chance to feed her family the often vitally needed vitamin C in a pleasant form. At that time vitamin tablets were unheard of, and scurvy took its yearly toll. Great mounds of preserves were put away every fall to meet the needs of a long winter and spring.

To us late comers, the dessert is like money in the bank; something extra when another not so interesting meal has been served and we can always hope that a good dessert or cake will save the meal.

Sugar was often expensive and hard to come by, and its use was restricted to important occasions. Maple sugar was often used in places where it could be had.

I can remember as a young lad on our farm, when on Saturdays the sugar chest was brought out containing the sugar top, one piece of solid sugar about two feet tall and ten inches in diameter at the bottom, formed as a cone. Then the tedious work of cutting this solid piece of sugar into serving size lumps began. Of course the granulated brown sugar was bought in one hundred pound bags and kept under lock and key. When the bags were empty they were turned into dish towels. Those days are long gone; we think nothing now of spilling a cup of sugar on the floor and sweeping it into the garbage.

How differently we live today! Whether things are better now or worse, I leave to you, my readers, to determine.

SETTLERS' DELIGHT GINGERBREAD CAKE

When we settled on our farmland, 150 years after the first settlers had claimed the land, we were welcomed by our neighbors in the same way as has been the custom in this part of the country since the first settlers arrived.

On one of the first of many rainy, cold mornings that fall, when our spirits were low, our neighbors Raymond and Rose Free appeared like rays of sunshine carrying the loveliest gingerbread cake we had ever tasted. We called this marvellous cake "Settler's Delight" and here is the recipe as given to us by Mrs. Free.

1 cup shortening	1½ teaspoons ginger
½ cup brown sugar	½ teaspoon salt
2 eggs, beaten	¾ teaspoon soda
½ cup table molasses	1 teaspoon baking powder
1½ cups pastry flour	½ cup boiling water

Put the shortening in a large mixing bowl and cream. Add the sugar and beat well. Add the eggs and molasses stirring constantly. Sprinkle the flour, ginger, salt, soda and baking powder on top of the mix. Add the boiling water and mix well quickly but do not over mix.

Preheat the oven to 350 degrees F. Grease a large baking dish with butter, add the mix and bake in the oven for 30 minutes. Check for doneness by inserting a skewer in the middle of the cake. If it comes out dry, the cake is ready. Remove from the oven and cool in the baking pan.

APPLE MUFFINS

I still remember from my childhood these wonderful muffins which were made only for festive occasions on our farm, particularly in the early fall when fresh fruit had started to ripen.

5 tablespoons butter	**1¼ cups flour**
½ cup sugar	**½ teaspoon baking powder**
1 egg	

Cream the butter and sugar by beating them against the sides of the bowl with a wooden spoon until light and fluffy. Beat the egg. Sift the flour and baking powder together and add to the butter-egg mixture using your fingers to blend all the ingredients into a soft dough. Shape into a ball, wrap in wax paper and place in the refrigerator for at least one hour.

Preheat the oven to 350 degrees F. Grease a twelve-muffin tin with butter, cut off one-third of the chilled dough and set aside. Divide the rest of the dough into twelve equal pieces and press each piece firmly to the bottom and sides of the muffin tin. The dough lining should be about one-quarter inch thick.

Fill each pastry cup with two tablespoons of filling. (See below.)

Roll out the remaining dough on a floured pastry board to about one-eighth of an inch thickness. Use a glass or a cookie cutter to cut the dough into twelve circles of the same diameter as the muffin cups. Moisten the edges of the filled muffins and place the tops on, pressing firmly around the edges to make a complete seal between the tops and the muffin cups. Bake in the middle of the oven for 45 minutes. Remove from the oven and cool in the muffin tin. Use a thin table knife to loosen muffins before taking them out of the tin.

FILLING:

2 tart cooking apples, cored	**2 tablespoons butter**
peeled and diced	**slivered almonds**

Melt the butter in a saucepan over moderate heat and add the finely chopped apples. Cook for 2 to 3 minutes, shaking the pan to cover the apples in the butter. Use for above recipe.

SOUR CREAM POUND CAKE

When visiting the Finn-Jones settlement in northern Ontario we had a sour cream pound cake which was delicious. Here is the recipe.

2 teaspoons butter, softened	**1 teaspoon soda**
1 tablespoon dry bread crumbs	**1 teaspoon ground cinnamon**
8 tablespoons softened butter	**1 teaspoon ground cardamom**
1 cup maple sugar	**1 cup sour cream**
3 eggs	**1 teaspoon vanilla**
1¼ cups all-purpose flour	

Melt the butter in a high nine by five-inch loaf pan. Swish the melted butter around the pan or brush it onto the sides with a pastry brush. Sprinkle the bottom and sides with the bread crumbs.

Tap out any excess crumbs and set aside. Preheat the oven to 350 degrees F.

Cream the butter with the powdered maple sugar by beating vigorously against the sides of the bowl with a wooden spoon until the mixture is light and fluffy. Beat in the eggs one at a time, making sure that each one is thoroughly mixed before the next is added. Sift together the flour, soda, cinnamon and cardamom and stir into the batter. Beat in the sour cream and vanilla. Make sure that the mixture is well mixed.

Pour the contents of the bowl into the breaded loaf pan. Rap the pan sharply against the table to remove any air bubbles in the mixture. Bake for one hour or until the top of the cake is golden brown.

Check for doneness by inserting a skewer in the middle of the cake. If it comes out dry, the cake is ready. Run a table knife around the sides of the pan to free the cake, then cool in the baking pan. When partly cool transfer to a cake rack and let cool completely.

PASTRY CONES FILLED WITH BERRIES

It was the custom in our family that on our birthdays we could choose our menu, and for many years this dish was my birthday wish.

2 eggs	1 cup chilled heavy cream
¼ cup superfine sugar	1 tablespoon sugar
3 tablespoons flour	1 teaspoon vanilla
2 teaspoons butter	¾ cup lingonberries, or
1 tablespoon flour	fresh strawberries

Preheat the oven to 400 degrees F. In a large bowl beat together the eggs and sugar until they are thoroughly combined. Stir in the flour, a little at a time, and mix until smooth.

Grease a cookie sheet sparingly and sprinkle with flour, tipping the sheet to make an even covering. Tap off any excess flour. Place two tablespoons of the batter on the cookie sheet and with the back of a large spoon, spread the batter out in a circle of about a four-inch diameter. I usually get four circles on each sheet. Bake in the middle of the oven for about 8 minutes, or until the circles are golden brown around the edges. Free the circles from the sheet with a knife, and quickly form a cone. Have several empty water glasses ready to stand the cones in. Let the cones stand in the glasses until cold. Then they can be moved and still keep their shape. Just before the cones are to be served, put the heavy cream in a chilled mixing bowl. Whip the cream with a wire whisk or a rotary beater until it begins to thicken. Add the sugar and vanilla and continue to beat until firm enough to hold its shape.

Spoon the whipped cream into the cones and top each with lingonberries or one strawberry. Place the cones in a water glass and serve as soon as possible.

BAKED APPLES

This is another one of my favorite desserts from my days as a boy on the farm.

2 cups cold water	¼ pound butter, softened
¼ lemon	¾ cup sugar
6 large tart cooking apples	1 tablespoon cinnamon
½ cup sugar	3 egg yolks
2 teaspoons soft butter	½ cup ground almonds
	3 egg whites

In a two-quart saucepan combine the cold water, the juice of the lemon and the lemon quarter itself.

Peel the apples and core with a tube corer. Place in the saucepan with the lemon water to prevent discoloration. Stir in the sugar and let come to a boil over medium heat. Lower the heat and simmer for 10 minutes. Remove from heat and drain on a rack. Preheat the oven to 350 degrees F. With a pastry brush, grease a shallow baking dish just large enough to hold the six apples. Place the apples side by side with the holes up. Cream the one-quarter pound of butter with the sugar by beating against the sides with a wooden spoon until light and fluffy.

Add the cinnamon and egg yolks. When the mixture is smooth and creamy, fill the holes in the apples with the mixture.

Smear the top with what is left over. With a wire whisk, beat the egg whites until they form stiff unwavering peaks. Spread the egg whites over the apples and sprinkle the almonds on top. Bake in the oven for 20 minutes or until the surface is golden. Remove from heat and cool to room temperature before serving.

BERRY PUDDING

This dessert always surprises and pleases my dinner guests. It was first served to me in a small homestead in northern Alberta on a hot summer day.

½ cup uncooked cream-of-wheat **3 cups cranberry juice**
6 tablespoons sugar

In a two-quart saucepan, bring the cranberry juice to a boil over moderate heat. Add the sugar, stirring constantly. Add the cream-of-wheat a little at a time, stirring briskly with a wooden spoon. Reduce the heat and simmer for 10 minutes until the mixture has thickened to a purée.

Transfer the mixture to a large mixing bowl. Using a rotary beater, beat the mixture until it has tripled in volume, and is very light and fluffy. Pour into individual serving bowls and serve as soon as possible.

NOTE: You can use apple, strawberry or raspberry juice by adding one teaspoon lemon juice.

WILD STRAWBERRY BREAD PUDDING

This early summer dish is delightful, and after a day of hard labor picking the wild strawberries you appreciate the pudding even more.

2 quarts wild strawberries **12 slices homemade-style**
2 cups superfine sugar   **white bread**
         2 cups heavy cream

Pick over the wild strawberries carefully, removing any that are bruised. Wash in a large sieve under running cold water.

Shake the berries dry. Place in a large mixing bowl and sprinkle the sugar on top. Toss the berries very gently with a large spoon until all the sugar has dissolved. Cover the berries and set aside.

Cut a slice of bread to fit the bottom of a deep two-quart bowl. Cut eight or nine slices of bread into wedges about four inches at the top and three inches across the bottom. Line the sides of the bowl with the wedges, overlapping each one by about one-half inch. Pour the fruit into the bowl and cover the top completely with the rest of the bread. Cover the top of the bowl with a flat plate and place a weight on top of the plate. Refrigerate for at least 12 hours.

Remove the mold by placing a chilled serving plate upside down on the bowl and inverting it. The mold should slide out easily.

Whip the cream in a large bowl until it holds its shape. With a rubber spatula, cover the the mold on the outside and top. Using a cake decorator set, decorate with curls and roses. Serve chilled.

STELLA'S APPLE STRUDEL

Not very often does one find an apple strudel as good as the one Stella Sanders makes. Stella is the wife of the artist who has done so much to enhance this book. We meet quite often over a pleasant meal and here is one of Stella's specialties.

2 eggs, beaten	2 tablespoons sliced citron
1½ tablespoons softened butter	¼ cup currants
1 cup sifted flour	½ cup sugar
4 tablespoons butter	¼ teaspoon cinnamon
4 apples, pared and sliced thin	1 tablespoon butter
½ cup almonds, blanched and cut thin	

In a large mixing bowl, combine the eggs and softened butter. Beat well. Add the flour a little at a time making sure that the mixture is well blended. Roll dough out on floured wax paper, making sure that the dough is paper thin, (thin enough to see through). Place the apples, almonds and citron on the dough. Spread with currants, then with sugar and cinnamon and dot with butter.

Roll the filled dough as you would a jelly roll. Preheat the oven to 350 degrees F. Put the dough and fruit roll in a long baking dish. Dot with the four tablespoons of butter and bake until nicely browned, about 30 minutes. Serve cold with whipped cream.

YOGURT

One of the biggest problems the early settlers had was how to keep milk sweet for any length of time without refrigeration. Yogurt was often eaten as a dessert with the everyday meal, as a milk substitute.

Yogurt is a cultured milk product made with *lactobacillus bulgaricus* and has been known to man since Biblical times. One of the wonderful things about yogurt is that it can be made from cow, goat, buffalo, reindeer, mare or ewe milk.

Yogurt culture was guarded as carefully as sourdough starter.

You can still make your own yogurt, but now you have to go a health food store to buy the culture. Once you have the starter made you can go on forever and make your own yogurt. Here is how to begin.

1 quart whole pasteurized milk	1/3 ounce dry Bulgarian culture

In a two-quart saucepan, heat the milk to 180 degrees F. A thermometer is useful but I have often made yogurt without one in the bush. Cool the milk to about 100 degrees. Stir in the culture and mix well. Pour the mixture into small soup bowls or into one big bowl. Cover the bowl with clear plastic wrap and set in a warm place. I use a small wooden box in which I have installed a light socket with a fifteen watt bulb. If I am in the bush I usually place the milk in a quart jar and bury the bottle in the dying ashes of my campfire.

Whatever method is used, it is vitally important that the mixture is left undisturbed for at least 5 hours, sometimes as long as 10 hours. Remove from the box and put in a cool place; a refrigerator if you are at home, or in a cold stream if on the trail.

Successive batches can be made by saving a small part of the yogurt to be used as a starter for the next batch.

YOGURT WITH CRANBERRIES

1 quart yogurt, chilled   1 teaspoon cinnamon
1 teaspoon sugar   1 cup cranberries

Beat the yogurt in a large bowl until thick and creamy. Add the sugar and cinnamon. Mix well, then add the cranberries, stir well and serve chilled.

YOGURT IN SOUP BOWLS

4 soup bowls yogurt   4 teaspoons cinnamon
4 teaspoons sugar

Make the yogurt in soup bowls and cool in the refrigerator for at least 3 hours. Sprinkle sugar and cinnamon on top and serve chilled.

INDEX

189